THE HANDBOOK FOR
ORGANIZATIONAL CHANGE

Strategy and skill for trainers and developers

Latest titles in the McGraw-Hill Training Series

DESIGNING AND ACHIEVING COMPETENCY
A Competency Based Approach to Developing People and
Organizations
Editors: Rosemary Boam
and Paul Sparrow   ISBN 0-07-707572-2

TOTAL QUALITY TRAINING
The Quality Culture and Quality Trainer
Brian Thomas   ISBN 0-07-707472-6

CAREER DEVELOPMENT AND PLANNING
A Guide for Managers, Trainers and Personnel Staff
Malcolm Peel   ISBN 0-07-707554-4

SALES TRAINING
A Guide to Developing Effective Sales People
Frank S. Salisbury   ISBN 0-07-707458-0

CLIENT-CENTRED CONSULTING
A Practical Guide for Internal Advisers and Trainers
Peter Cockman, Bill Evans
and Peter Reynolds   ISBN 0-07-707685-0

TRAINING TO MEET THE TECHNOLOGY CHALLENGE
Trevor Bentley   ISBN 0-07-707589-7

IMAGINATIVE EVENTS Volumes I & II
Ken Jones   ISBN 0-07-707679-6 Volume I
                ISBN 0-07-707680-X Volume II
                ISBN 0-07-707681-8 for set of Volumes I & II

LEARNING THROUGH SIMULATIONS
A Guide to the Design and Use of Simulations in Business and Education
John Fripp   ISBN 0-07-707588-9

MEETINGS MANAGEMENT
Leslie Rae   ISBN 07-707782-2

WORKSHOPS THAT WORK
Tom Bourner, Vivien Martin
and Phil Race   ISBN 0-07-707800-4

TRAINING FOR PROFIT
Philip Darling   ISBN 0-07-707785-7

Details of these and other titles in the series are available from:

The Product Manager, Professional Books, McGraw-Hill Book Company Europe,
Shoppenhangers Road, Maidenhead, Berkshire, SL6 2QL.
Telephone: 0628 23432 Fax: 0628 770224

Edinburgh Napier University

Customer name: DANIELLA ERICA KALVELID

Customer ID: ^^^^^^^^^^^2534

Title: The handbook for organizational change : strategy and skill for trainers and developers /
ID: 38042001734761
Due: 23/11/2015 23:59:00 GMT

Items that you renewed

Title: The theory and practice of change management /
ID: 38042007228529
Due: 02/11/2015 23:59:00 GMT

Title: Managing change in organizations /
ID: 38042008784546
Due: 02/11/2015 23:59:00 GMT

Title: Entrepreneurship and small firms /
ID: 38042008920009
Due: 02/11/2015 23:59:00 GMT

Title: Managing change in organizations /
ID: 38042007115445
Due: 02/11/2015 23:59:00 GMT

Total items: 5
25/10/2015   13:39
Overdue: 0
Hold requests: 0

The handbook for organizational change

Strategy and skill for trainers and developers

Carol A. O'Connor PhD

McGRAW-HILL BOOK COMPANY

London · New York · St Louis · San Francisco · Auckland
Bogotá · Caracas · Lisbon · Madrid · Mexico · Milan
Montreal · New Delhi · Panama · Paris · San Juan · São Paulo
Singapore · Sydney · Tokyo · Toronto

Published by
McGRAW-HILL Book Company Europe
Shoppenhangers Road, Maidenhead, Berkshire SL6 2QL, England.
Telephone 0628 23432
Fax 0628 770224

British Library Cataloguing in Publication Data
O'Connor, Carol A.
  Handbook of Organizational Change:
  Strategy and Skill for Trainers and
  Developers. – (McGraw-Hill Training
  Series)
  I. Title   II. Series
  658.4

  ISBN 0-07-707693-1

Library of Congress Cataloging-in-Publication Data
O'Connor, Carol A.,
    The handbook for organizational change : strategy and skill for
  trainers and developers / Carol A. O'Connor.
        p.   cm.—(McGraw-Hill training series)
    Includes bibliographical references and index.
    ISBN 0-07-707693-1
    1. Organizational change—Handbooks, manuals, etc. 2. Strategic
  planning—Handbooks, manuals, etc.   I. Title.   II. Series.
  HD58.8.O27   1993
    658.4'06—dc20   93-21715
                                                                 CIP

12345 CL 96543

Typeset by Book Ens Limited, Baldock, Herts
Printed and bound in Great Britain by Clays, Ltd.

Contents

Series preface

Training and development are now firmly centre stage in most organizations, if not all. Nothing unusual in that—for some organizations. They have always seen training and development as part of the heart of their businesses—but more and more must see it the same way.

The demographic trends through the 1990s will inject into the marketplace severe competition for good people who will need good training. Young people without conventional qualifications, skilled workers in redundant crafts, people out of work, women wishing to return to work—all will require excellent training to fit them to meet the job demands of the 1990s and beyond.

But excellent training does not spring from what we have done well in the past. T&D specialists are in a new ball game. 'Maintenance' training—training to keep up skill levels to do what we have always done—will be less in demand. Rather, organization, work and market change training are now much more important and will remain so for some time. Changing organizations and people is no easy task, requiring special skills and expertise which, sadly, many T&D specialists do not possess.

To work as a 'change' specialist requires us to get to centre stage—to the heart of the company's business. This means we have to ask about future goals and strategies and even be involved in their development, at least as far as T&D policies are concerned.

This demands excellent communication skills, political expertise, negotiating ability, diagnostic skills—indeed, all the skills a good internal consultant requires.

The implications for T&D specialists are considerable. It is not enough merely to be skilled in the basics of training, we must also begin to act like business people and to think in business terms and talk the language of business. We must be able to resource training not just from within but by using the vast array of external resources. We must be able to manage our activities as well as any other manager. We must share in the creation and communication of the company's vision. We must never let the goals of the company out of our sight.

In short, we may have to grow and change with the business. It will be hard. We shall not only have to demonstrate relevance but also value for money and achievement of results. We shall be our own boss, as accountable for results as any other line manager, and we shall have to deal with fewer internal resources.

The challenge is on, as many T&D specialists have demonstrated to me over the past few years. We need to be capable of meeting that challenge. This is why McGraw-Hill Book Company Europe have planned and launched this major new training series—to help us meet that challenge.

The series covers all aspects of T&D and provides the knowledge base from which we can develop plans to meet the challenge. They are practical books for the professional person. They are a starting point for planning our journey into the twenty-first century.

Use them well. Don't just read them. Highlight key ideas, thoughts, action pointers or whatever, and have a go at doing something with them. Through experimentation we evolve; through stagnation we die.

I know that all the authors in the McGraw-Hill Training Series would want me to wish you good luck. Have a great journey into the twenty-first century.

ROGER BENNETT
Series Editor

Preface

It is a paradox that acceptance of change creates stability while resistance to it produces chaos. As a consultant and trainer in business, I am fascinated by this. When managers rigidly hold on to the successes of the past, they become unable to produce new achievements in the future. Having a flexible attitude and self-awareness are as important as using a system and method when managing change.

This book emphasizes both. It offers a four-stage method for managing change and also describes how to lead change initiatives and manage resistance when it occurs. All of the techniques, example problems, case studies and the highlighted concepts recommend understanding the unique needs of each change situation. Managers benefit most when they accept and value different or new ideas. Too often, 'discrimination' and 'judgement' mean saying 'no'. The approach presented here suggests openness to change and a creative response to alternative points of view.

The seven chapters follow a similar format throughout. In each, a case study based on the experience of a business manager highlights the issues to be raised in that chapter. The chapters' content is application-oriented, with extensive use of examples. Activities are presented which guide an analysis of the ideas put forward. There is a problem, with follow-up questions, and a discussion in each chapter to illustrate the kind of business situation which would benefit from the concepts offered.

The table of contents provides a detailed outline of each chapter. Readers are advised to use this and the index as guides for exploring specific topics of interest to them. When reference is made to ideas or activities raised in previous chapters, page numbers are provided for readers of the 'dip and browse' school of business book reading. In this way, they can choose to read those sections most relevant to their needs.

For many years I studied the Japanese martial art, Aikido. One practice technique requires a single student to stand encircled by opponents. As they attack, the student fends them off, using ever-changing manoeuvres against their unpredictable and random blows. What is most noticeable about this dynamic display is the calm facial expression and the steady physical rhythm of the students most proficient at this technique. Although moving rapidly, they appear to be quiet, balanced and completely secure.

The seven managers interviewed for the case studies in this book all demonstrate a similar ability: to express calm and concentration in situations of challenge, turbulence or widespread change. These managers come from a variety of backgrounds, industries and countries, and each demonstrates different qualities as managers of change, but all are equally pro-active. They cooperate with events and people rather than seek to control them. I would like to thank them for their candour, their interest and especially their time—a valued gift from busy people. They are: Cathy Carter Duncan, Ian Halliday, Tina Kaplan, Tony Lewis, Daniel Ofman, Paull Robathan and Steve Tanner. Their companies' addresses are listed in the Appendix.

I also thank George and Judith Brown and Stewart Shapiro whose ideas very much influence this approach to change management. Finally, I offer heartfelt thanks to Margaret, Marilyn and Jean O'Connor and Jerry Maserjian whose support made the writing of this book possible.

1 Method and skills

The need for quality

Thirty years ago, industrial decisions were primarily based on the ideas of then-called 'captains of industry'. Manufacturers and suppliers of services held enormous control over the market place as their customers' demand for new products, inventions and services exceeded the available supply. The business world actually influenced public taste and fashion with considerable success. Gradually, this situation changed. With the growth of international markets, satellite communication and increasingly swift transportation, companies began to face global as well as local and national competition.

In the last years of this century, the customer has gained control of the market place. This dramatic shift of power is perhaps the logical end result of the 200 year-old industrial revolution. After all, consumer sophistication results from technological advance. Their easy access to manufactured goods contributes to present-day increases in competition.

Business leaders respond to this power shift in a variety of ways. Some ignore it and carry on producing goods as if nothing has changed since the war, that is, the Second World War. Others respond with scientific and rational approaches. They give 'systems analysis', 'strategic planning', 'rationalization' and other business methods almost mystical power within their boardrooms, the basic principle of their approach being that problems are solved by finding a cause and applying the right solution.

A third group of leaders recognize that they must respond directly to this change in consumer attitude. Having listened to their customers, they initiate 'customer focus', 'customer is king', 'quality first', 'total quality excellence', and many other related initiatives. They believe that consumers are likely to choose companies which serve them better with top quality goods and services. Further, these customers are likely to stay with those companies which do this consistently. Their quality programmes aim to attract and to keep business.

Those companies which actively pursue quality initiatives create a momentum for healthy growth into the next century. This is fact, not conjecture. Competition is now too severe, with customer requirements too high for leaders to be driven by personal whim, empire building for its own sake, and short-term profiteering. Hence the urgency among knowledgeable leaders to be the first and the best with quality and other customer-driven initiatives.

This book is for these leaders and managers. They already realize that change is now inevitable. They also know that it is wide-sweeping and a challenge. Having accepted these points, they are faced with the enormous complexity of managing company-wide change. While experience, training and skill go a long way towards guiding these leaders, they also benefit from a handbook which outlines a system for managing change successfully.

Company-wide standard

This system must be generic and apply equally to the boardroom and to the shop floor. This is because many boardroom decisions have a direct impact on the shop floor and its operators. A company-wide standard for guiding the process of change leads to a shared responsibility for making change happen. It is so much more efficient to require all company levels—from senior managers to hourly-paid workers—to base decisions about change on analysis of data and informed discussion. A common system leads to a common language and easier application of new ideas throughout the company.

This challenges the old-fashioned idea that social class determines where and how people work and that different rules apply to these different classes. Companies which attempt to enforce such class division cannot survive. General education, television and politics have changed forever the way people think about work and their employers. Wise company leaders show their employees appropriate respect when they ask everyone to use the same guidelines when managing change. It is this respect more than higher salaries which inspires employees' commitment.

Everyone in the company should be asked to consider the company's future as if they are members of the board. They should also be expected to give attention to the quality of each task as if they operate its machines or answer its phones. Those leaders who set high company-wide standards for change management also create a framework for a company-wide quality programme. Effective, efficient change management is one aspect of life in the excellent company.

The need for vision

Much is written about corporate culture and yet there is still widespread confusion about what this term actually means. Essentially, culture, atmosphere, and company customs develop over a period of time and result from the way people habitually act toward one another in the course of their work. These patterns of behaviour are usually initiated at the company's formation. As the company ages, they become increasingly difficult to alter.

Those leaders who ignore company culture when they initiate change do so at their peril. Change which radically affects current culture is very difficult to implement. Even when there is goodwill and the desire to cooperate, habit and long-standing attitudes inhibit employees from adjusting to new ideas.

Leaders need to offer a powerful vision for future change as an antidote to ingrained routine. Concurrently, they should also acknowledge that the company's past and present achievements have led to the present new efforts. This vision must be an integration of the hopes, dreams and ambitions of those responsible for the company and also promise practical benefit for the company as a whole. Leaders need to describe their vision for any new venture or proposal so that it inspires their colleagues to implement the change. It is vision which creates continued support and commitment for a project during the inevitable periods of disruption and discomfort. While an organized and systematic approach ensures effective management of change, a vision encourages company employees to want the change to occur.

Creating vision can seem a formidable assignment to some leaders. It becomes easier once they remember that everyone has some vision for the future. Although it is often difficult to express, a vision answers the question, 'What would I like the future to hold for this company?' Leaders who have a clear response to this question, and who are able to listen to the responses of others, serve everyone within the company.

Clarity from the top allows everyone at every level to be more creative and productive. When people know where the company is going, they are able to contribute to this direction. If they are confused about company priorities, they can gradually lose interest in performing their best. It is a soul-destroying experience to work conscientiously to complete a project only to learn that top leaders have changed their mind about what they want or made a mistake about the project's needs. If miscommunication is a company-wide habit, employees lose respect for their leaders and certainly do not exert themselves on their behalf.

Company priorities The success of any change depends on whether the people involved are willing to alter their behaviour in order to achieve a company priority. There is potential difficulty when a company promotes one priority, but in fact supports another. While there is no quick fix for this situation, closing the gap between verbal and actual priorities is an essential task for leaders of change.

Company purpose Discovery of gaps between verbal and actual priorities is a first step when clarifying company vision. Pretending that gaps don't exist is a mistake because this undermines management credibility. When everyone knows that 'Cost-saving comes first', the statement 'Quality comes first' presented as a company priority simply makes employees laugh.

It is essential to decide company priorities and these must be based on company purpose. This, of course, is not an easy task. For example, those companies owned by shareholders have a legal responsibility to conserve their investors' interests. Even assuming long-term or intangible

Activity 1 1 Does the company have a mission statement? If so, what is it?
2 As a manager of change, what would you list as company priorities?
3 Are you aware of any gaps between actual everyday priorities and those expressed in the company mission or by company leaders?
4 Imagine yourself to be in the role of the *least* influential person in the company. What would you list as the company priorities from that point of view?
5 Imagine yourself to be in the role of the *most* influential person in your company. What would you list as the company priorities from that point of view?

benefit, company leaders must ask whether these interests include an expensive environmental protection initiative or, alternatively, a cost-saving but unsafe machinery purchase.

Company leaders can feel themselves in a double dilemma: they must stay in profit and also produce quality products. It takes careful planning and complete commitment to long-term success to integrate these two requirements. If, in the past, pressure to increase profit undermined quality, leaders must acknowledge this if they want to create a new vision for the future. Otherwise, their staff and even their customers will not believe them when they insist on a renewed statement of company priorities that 'Quality comes first at XYZ Corporation'.

The method for managing change presented in these pages is most useful when leaders offer a clear vision for the company's future. Only then can they and their managers plan and implement new ideas. The techniques offered in stage one of this method, 'Identifying change', can guide production of a company vision (see page 18, Chapter 2). Although the suggestions refer to goal-setting, they also apply to creation of the company's over-arching goals—its vision.

Articulation of company purpose and priorities leads to unity. When these express a commitment to inspiring values, then this encourages positive and wholesome action from company members. It is necessary for those at the top to strive to close the gap between vision and reality. Quality products are the result of integrating vision and practice.

Bias against planning

It must be said that there are strong biases against planning and against a systematic approach. Some of this negative feeling directly results from the behaviour of those leaders who so strongly emphasize strategic planning and systems thinking. This is unfortunate, because plans which are based on reality and inspired by vision provide excitement and generate commitment throughout a company. Staff contribute far more to a company when its leaders tell them where it is going and invite them to suggest better ways of getting there.

There is certainly enough research available to convince the most cynical manager that people want and need to feel some control over what they do. Sharing plans for the company's future is virtually impossible if none are developed. It is even more unrealistic to ask staff to contribute to creating future plans if company leaders do not know how to integrate their good ideas into a plan or how tactfully to refuse any impractical ones.

Managers set themselves up for bad feeling and low morale among staff when they ask for ideas and then ignore what is offered. Rightly or wrongly, staff and colleagues imagine they are being manipulated. Successful change initiatives should be based on *use of planning method* as well as *skills for managing people*. Managers who are familiar with both can address problems as they arise and manage change so that the needs of the company are best served without alienating employees.

Team-building for change

Final responsibility for change often rests on the shoulders of one person, but no single manager realistically creates company-wide change. Long-term decisions are made at the highest levels, but these leaders depend on others to produce the change. They need team leadership skills as much as, if not more than, the supervisors of clerical staff or of machine operators who actually implement their ideas for change. Planning technique, together with people skills, are requirements for managing change effectively. This applies to senior managers as they delegate projects to others and equally to those who complete the projects in a cascade throughout the company.

Many of the most disastrous decisions appearing in the financial news are made at director-level by people who are not even interested in how or whether their decisions can be implemented. They argue with hindsight that their task is to maintain the company's place in the market. They suggest that other issues and internal company business matters are less vital and are the responsibility of operational managers. This view is actually a narrow and limited one although it sounds wide and magisterial.

Effective company directors know how to shift their attention from external to internal company issues. They ask for regular and briefly presented reports about internal affairs and they know how to request this information so that it is timely and useful when it arrives. Their success is based on good relationships between themselves and other levels of management.

Leaders who want their companies to succeed bring a quality-first attitude to their own performance. This means a team attitude that is more than a slogan about pulling together. They also model the professionalism they want others to exhibit, and inspire the company with vision and practical schemes. Their challenge is to think 'expansive' and 'big' about the company's future and 'specific' and 'detailed' about its present reality.

This principle applies to operational managers as well. Any choice for change should take into account the greater needs of the company as a whole. The task is to envision solutions which contribute positively to the company's larger vision. When these managers are delegated implementation of a major change, they need the support of all their colleagues and staff. It takes team leadership skill to present a vision of change so that everyone wants to contribute to it and make it happen. The greater the sense of team, the more likely it is that change occurs within budget and with least disruption to 'business as usual'.

Team work doesn't happen automatically, nor does it result from the occasional rousing speech from an otherwise unavailable manager or company managing director. 'In the old days', some leaders say, 'it was easy. I said jump to it and they did. So why do people need a lot of hand-holding now?' There is no simple answer to this. One possible response would be to remind them of the complexity of business today and the increased threat of competition.

Wrong decisions can be extremely expensive at best, and catastrophic at worst. If managers can gain information and insight about the company from its employees, then they would be wise to take advantage of this. But this source can only be tapped by creating a sense of team, not by saying 'jump to it'. Employees may jump, but they won't necessarily jump as far or as high as they are capable. Companies today need more than obedient servants, they need cooperation, commitment and good ideas.

A cautionary tale

This is a story which illustrates the need for a systematic approach to change management. Its circumstantial details are completely altered to maintain client confidentiality.

In mid-1990, a senior manager scheduled a business counselling session with a consultant. He wanted to replay a series of events in order to analyse them and discover how he could improve his performance in a similar situation in the future. In January of that same year, Bob—not his real name—was invited to join a highly secret and select investigating panel by one of the company's world-sector presidents of operations. This panel was multi-level among senior grades and included 15 specialists. Its brief was to explore solutions to the company's increasingly serious cash-flow crisis. The cash shortage threatened to cripple the company's entire world-wide operation.

During the next six months, the panel researched key issues with both effectiveness and efficiency and finally produced a comprehensive report. The panel chairman, a Machiavellian character, thanked the panellists at the project's finish but explained that politically the recommendations they proposed would negatively affect him by hurting his own division. Because this, in turn, would damage the company as a whole, their recommendations would have to be changed.

Bob, middle-aged but still an idealist, was angered by this and gave an ultimatum that the report should stand as it was or he would resign. Coolly, the chairman replied, 'Resign and I'll finish you in this company.' This message was absorbed with equal attention by the other 13 panellists. The end result was a radically doctored report finally reaching the president. Two years later, the financial press is full of news about this company's extensive redundancies and a take-over battle which its leaders won at tremendous cost to the company. The panel chairman, on the other hand, moved to a vice-president's position in a rival company and recently accepted a non-executive directorship on a major company's board.

This story offers an example of a sincere and determined wish for change from the highest company levels. This was short-circuited by company members who lacked courage, integrity or, in the case of Bob, skill to manage change amidst controversy. Although they let their company down badly, the president himself also let the panellists down. Why didn't he question whether this group of experts was lying to him to serve their own ends? What action did he take to ensure that the advice they gave was substantially correct with minimum omission? Why didn't he realize that sincerity and good intentions lack any influence when proposed change poses a big enough threat to special interests? Careful preparation is always needed to prevent sabotage.

Change management requires special skills because by its very nature change brings the unexpected. This is particularly true of radical change. Conscientious managers gain little comfort if they discover later that their change initiative failed because a group of panellists lied. Instead, they ask themselves, 'Why didn't I see this coming?' Of course, they feel worse if they actually discover that the project failed because they lied to themselves.

The challenge—and it is an exciting one—is to create change with such clarity that it is bound to succeed, or if not succeed, at least contribute some lasting positive good to the company. This can be achieved by using a methodical approach, by leading with intelligence and by managing resistance as it occurs. This book presents these three topics, essential to effective change management.

Four-stage method

When contaminants are found in a water supply, a crucial manufacturing line breaks down, or a parts supplier suddenly goes into receivership, leaders must take immediate action. They think on their feet, organize as they speak and monitor results as events occur. The experience, training and background of those managing this kind of change contribute to the effort's success.

When asked about change management, many managers give examples of creating change while under fire. For that reason it is worthwhile to examine if there is any similarity between the emergency situation and planned company initiatives, such as moving corporate headquarters or making redundant an entire level of management. Are the skills of managing fast action as events move rapidly the same as those required for planning and implementing company-wide innovation?

At first glance the two situations seem very different, but in both cases experienced managers organize people and resources to create new and different circumstances. They think; they plan; they initiate. This book suggests that the differences between change through crisis and change through strategic planning are superficial. Certainly some managers are more effective when handling crisis than others. They bring special skills to the situation. Also, others have long-term planning skills and they excel at coordinating non-crisis company change. While the specific skills needed to manage these change efforts differ, change itself is essentially the same.

This book suggests that change of any type is best managed systematically. In times of crisis, this is done so rapidly that it often appears that leaders make random or lucky stroke decisions. The application of method is more obvious in planned change initiatives. Even so, there is logic underlying any successfully managed change effort. This book aims to present that logic as a four-stage method.

Any leader who has introduced organizational change understands how challenging this can be. An idea which promised 'guaranteed success' can readily become an 'unfortunate mistake' with hindsight. Major change means risk as well as benefit. It also means disruption to the lives and work of those who implement it. Some of these will protest that a proposed change is too radical while others will complain that it is far too conservative, and a larger number still will withhold their reactions entirely.

Managers who attempt to initiate change without a plan or system to direct its progress increase the likelihood of problems arising. Not only are there always unforeseen difficulties, there are also unpredictable situations which arise as a result of the change. The more complex the organization, the greater the potential for confusion when change is introduced.

A plan provides a means of organizing basic information about the change. As implementation begins, it provides a means of checking whether events are proceeding as expected. Monitoring a plan is considerably easier on any manager's nerves than gathering information about events as they occur without a clear idea of their possible outcome. Even crisis-oriented change gains benefit from the use of techniques which organize information systematically and with maximum efficiency.

The smallest company, as well as the largest, can experience complex problems as soon as change is introduced. Every organization develops an internal logic which regulates how work is done; influences how relationships are formed; and guides how managers behave. All of these factors and more must be considered when planning change. The four-stage method presented in these pages offers a comprehensive overview of what leaders need to do in order to make organizational change a success in the long term. It provides a system which encourages setting future goals and directions while paying close attention to present realities.

Much of this is based on common sense. Basically, this method for change promotes the idea that managers can create stability by blending routine with change. Particularly in turbulent situations, steady and determined progress can be made if a system is followed and a sense of routine is maintained. Structure, guidelines, and clear and consistent information are immeasurably appreciated by staff who are thrust into ambiguous and undefined situations. Leaders who resist system or planning should consider the needs of their colleagues and staff as well as their responsibility to innovate.

The four stages for managing change recommended in this book are:

1 Identify what needs to change (Chapter 2)
2 Consider the company context (Chapter 3)
3 Plan and implement the change (Chapter 4)
4 Evaluate results (Chapter 5)

Each is presented fully in the following four chapters.

Stage 1: identify change

Many organizations put least time and energy into this stage because what needs to change can seem so obvious. In fact, allocating time for identification of change is critically important. The 'obvious' solution is not always the best one or the most appropriate. If care is taken to identify in precise terms what needs to change, then implementing a plan for change has greater chance of success.

This stage is most useful in situations where time is available for analysis and review. It also serves crisis-related change in two ways. First, it gives managers a framework within which to assess emergency-made decisions later, when the crisis is past and time allows. Second, the steps to identify change can become automatic to experienced managers, who can then use them to analyse any crisis rapidly and more effectively.

Stage 2: consider company context

This stage provides a second level of analysis. Having identified what needs to change, managers assess their goals in terms of the impact they will have on the rest of the organization. This avoids creating initiatives which are beneficial for an isolated company area, but which actually contradict long-term goals for the company as a whole. Leaders must learn to shift their perspective from narrow and 'local' considerations to 'bigger' and company-wide concerns when they consider the larger context for change.

Stage 3: plan and implement

Although planning and implementation are two different functions, this stage includes them both, to emphasize that the two must be integrated. Too often, plans are made by one company group and then implemented by a different group with minimum communication between the two.

Plans must be based on company realities, and an understanding must exist between planners and implementers. The more influence that implementers have in the planning process, the greater the plan's chance for success.

Stage 4: evaluation   To gain maximum benefit from any change, a full evaluation should be made of its outcome. This stage suggests how to do this efficiently, and further, how to use the information from this analysis effectively. Chapter 5 presents this stage and offers guidelines for managers to design their own survey questionnaires. This information is included because surveys are valuable aids for managers. They allow anonymous gathering of data about the change from those who are involved. The company is enriched by feedback from its employees, and surveys are one source of this information.

Problem— analysis— discussion

Problem   A 20-year-old food service company has dominated its local market almost since it was founded. The 80-person firm has major contracts with schools, industry and health service authorities providing ready-to-heat meals and a wide range of vending machine products. By combining reasonable prices, wholesome food and consistent service, they maintain their position as local, first-choice caterers. Other firms either have too little capital to develop their service or lack the necessary expertise to offer realistic competition.

The company is owned and managed by its two directors, a husband and wife team. Neither are formally trained in business, but both draw on common sense and a solid understanding of the food service industry. In general, they divide company management in half, with the wife supervising internal company business and the husband handling sales and marketing.

Recently, a nationally known catering firm entered a bid for a very lucrative car manufacturer's canteen service. Although the national firm lost the contract, the local company directors learn informally that it was a close contest. Simultaneously, they discover that a French firm who have just won a similar canteen bid in the next county is also bidding for a contract with one of their own big clients.

Because their competition has always been local, the directors always felt confident about their success. They managed each competitive situation coolly and skilfully. Confronted by what they call 'outsiders', they begin to feel less sure of themselves. The husband, in his mid-sixties, wonders if he isn't too old for 'cut-throat' competition. His wife is also worried because one of their long-term supervisors has just resigned in order to take a higher level job with the national firm's new local office. Both company directors agree that their new rivals create an entirely different challenge for their company.

Analysis *Please take the role of a consultant who has been asked by the two directors for advice. Answer these questions as if preparing yourself for the first session with the directors.*

1 What does this company need most?
2 What biases and beliefs do they have about their competition? About their own company?
3 How can they discover the accuracy of these ideas?
4 Upon which teams can the directors depend?

Discussion This company needs a strategy to meet changing circumstances. The longer the directors delay analysing their situation and planning for it, the weaker their confidence and position will become. The imagined enemy is far more terrifying than the visible one. In fact, the company directors have every reason to believe they can maintain their current success. Their history in the community has been excellent. Not only do they know their markets, they have long-term relationships with their suppliers.

Although they believe that their two new competitors have advantages over them, the directors should examine this more closely. Size and national status can also be considered disadvantages. The directors can apply the same common sense attitude for winning bids against the big firms as they have against smaller ones. They clearly don't appreciate their own strengths and they undervalue the considerable business skill which made them local market leaders. These biases should be assessed and then resolved through planning.

The directors' most serious concern should be loss of their senior staff. The national firm is wise to recruit from the local firm because this gives them an immediate source of information about local markets and the local firm's formula for success. The directors should do everything they can to get the supervisor to return to their firm. This may require them to examine their management style, the person's advancement ambitions and salary needs. The directors' greatest strength against serious competition is their staff. This is a team they must be able to count upon. If they cannot rely on their staff's support, the directors should face how they themselves should change in order to inspire this support and gain a renewed commitment from their staff.

Other teams which could become allies are local business groups, suppliers and their current clients. Their long-standing relationships with these groups need assessment. The directors should ask themselves how they can improve relationships with these people. The outside firms have none of their local contacts. The directors can strengthen their operation base simply by maintaining present contacts and seeking ways to strengthen these. Good communication, a positive attitude and solid strategy for change can increase this company's business, even in the face of severe competition.

Summary

Increasing competition requires company leaders to look for ways to improve continuously their products and services. This chapter suggests that quality-oriented companies are those which recognize the need to manage change effectively and systematically. An inspiring vision for the future provides employees with a common purpose and sense of direction. This vision allows everyone to contribute to company growth as they implement plans for change.

The leaders' task is to discover ways to close the gap between their vision of a better future and their awareness of present reality. Although there is a justifiable bias against over-planning, a method and plan for change encourages creativity when employees are encouraged to offer their ideas and suggestions. Asking for feedback contributes to a team atmosphere within the company.

The method for managing change used at the top of the company can be used with equal success at other levels. A four-stage method for change management includes: identifying what needs to change, considering the company context, planning and implementation, and evaluating results.

Selected reading

Gainer, Leila J., 'Making the Competitive Connection', *Training and Development Journal*. September 1989, S1–30.

Galbraith, John K., *The New Industrial State*. London: Hamilton, 1967.

Handy, Charles, *Waiting for the Mountain to Move*. London: Hutchinson, 1990.

Kanter, Rosebeth Moss, *When Giants Learn To Dance*. London: Unwin Hyman, 1990.

Mintzberg, Henry and Quinn, James B., *The Strategy Process* (2nd ed.). Englewood Cliffs, NJ: Prentice-Hall, 1991.

Naisbitt, John, *Megatrends: Ten New Directions Transforming Our Lives*. London: MacDonald, 1984.

Pearce, John A. II and Robinson, B. Jr, *Strategic Management: Strategic Formulation and Implementation* (2nd ed.). Homewood, IL: Irwin, 1985.

Reich, R.B., 'The Real Economy', *The Atlantic Monthly*. February 1991, 35–52.

2 Identify change

**More speed—
less haste**

This chapter introduces the first stage in a method for managing change. It offers a *framework* for identifying what needs to change and *techniques* to discover potential difficulties. Decisions for change which are based solely on an educated guess or even on past experience ignore the possibility of hidden influences. The more relevant information that is available, the less chance of project failure as a result of unforeseen events. When the need for change is considered in a systematic way, this brings to light potential problems so that they can be resolved. In a great many companies change 'just happens', seemingly dictated by circumstances or current events. When managers react, their efforts address symptoms and surface difficulties rather than essential company issues or problems.

There are occasions when managers rush into a project believing that the proposed change is a matter of common sense and can be easily implemented. After innumerable delays, they are forced to admit that the need for change has been misunderstood. Identifying in precise terms what needs to change and why leads to knowledge about the depth and extent of a problem. This minimizes risk to decisions about change by uncovering hidden pitfalls in advance. A thorough, in-depth investigation can reveal that there is an elegant and simple solution to a long-standing problem. Systematic analysis gives change a chance of success.

Case study

**The Prudential
Assurance Company
Limited**

> **The purpose of this case study is to illustrate the importance of identifying change. The manager involved used time wisely to gather information from a variety of sources about the needs for change. Only then did he propose specific goals for extensive and division-wide change.**

In 1990, the senior management team of Prudential Life Administration created a mission statement which is supported by a 'Way of Life' policy. In this, they made a firm commitment to quality service. Their mission statement reads:

'OUR MISSION: We administer Prudential Assurance life business. Our purpose is to delight our customers by delivering a quality service, in a cost effective manner, through the contribution of everyone.'

The decision to put the customer first required a complete evaluation of the management and organizational structure. The management team asked Ian Halliday, Operations Development Manager, to coordinate a restructuring project for the Life Administration division at Reading. His task was to identify areas for change and provide an implementation plan to achieve it.

This change initiative was the biggest and farthest reaching in the 25-year history of the Reading office. Because the project was a pioneer effort which would influence other areas of the Prudential, the management team wanted 'to get it right'. Ian believed that the only way to do this would involve a thorough examination of the organization and its change issues. It would also require the cooperation of almost every manager.

He began by studying the minutes and notes from senior management discussions about quality and customer focus issues. Then, 'I went around and talked to everybody and anybody who had an input or role to play. After numerous long conversations, the elements of what makes the business tick emerged.'

Ian further explained, 'I placed a lot of emphasis on visual presentation of the proposed new organization and the method of change. Supporting this, I produced an enormous matrix, based on all the input, demonstrating the categories of activity and issues for project implementation. Not only could management see clearly through the complexity but it gave them confidence that we had identified all the possible problems and could control and resolve them. Twenty-eight sub-projects, almost all interrelated, were identified. My role was to act as a driver for some; others were delegated to separate project teams.'

The identification stage took three months from its inception to Ian's presentation to the management team of the proposals for change. 'The actual presentation was a compilation of the many interviews. Managers had known of the proposed changes in advance and what impact they would have on their area. What did surprise them was the size and scope of the project when they could see how the individual aspects of the change would work together.' Following a half-day's intensive debate, they agreed to act on the reorganization ideas. Their decision to implement widespread change allowed Life Administration to reduce overheads by over £1.5 million a year.

'To achieve this kind of change successfully, there needs to be clarity of vision and a commitment to it. Everyone needs to take it on board and test it for themselves. Even if the change is only one step at a time, it allows refinement of the vision and encourages people to contribute and own the change for themselves.'

Perceived needs for change

Every change effort begins with a perceived need to alter some aspect of the company. Because accuracy depends on the quality of leaders' perceptions, there is no guarantee that these 'perceived needs' are perfectly identified. Information can be analysed and all assumptions questioned, and the change can still be in error. No responsible leader launches a major change believing that it will fail, but hindsight can make the effort seem random, unplanned and obviously wrong. Vital pieces of information can be missed for the best reasons.

In the Prudential Assurance case study, Ian Halliday interviewed a great many of his co-workers toward discovering 'what makes the business tick'. Although he had his own opinion based on a long work history with the company, he knew that the inclusion of information from as many people as possible would benefit the change immeasurably.

Dependence on the opinions of just a few individuals limits a company's ability to adapt successfully to changing circumstances. Although the final decision about change in most companies rests with the company's senior management, these leaders are wise to solicit comments and suggestions from all levels within the company. The manager who listens to feedback from operators and support staff creates a valuable information source for decision-making. Who better knows about maintenance requirements for varying brands of equipment than the staff who have been running the different models for a number of years?

This applies to change on a smaller scale as well. A department manager, responsible for radically cutting overheads, can discover numerous solutions to the problem by asking for suggestions from members of the whole department. No manager is entirely aware of every detail involved in each job, but staff members who are delegated these tasks know all about them. By asking for ideas which support the cost-cutting, this manager develops a plan which is both realistic and more likely to be implemented.

Three kinds of change

Many managers believe that 'Change is change', and employ a one-size-fits-all approach to change management. Actually, effective plans are based on knowing *what kind of change* is required. Deciding this is the first step to systematic identification of what needs to change. There are three basic kinds of change: routine, improvement, and innovative. Each of these is described here.

Routine

This refers to change which is planned and built into company procedures. These changes are regular and provide a systematic aspect to work-flow and production. Because they are periodic, employees anticipate them and actually feel anxiety if they do not occur. *Examples*: annual equipment upgrade in high technology fields, staff rotation among airline flight crews and other high-stress work areas, retooling of machinery for seasonal orders in manufacturing, or increasing staff during peak production periods.

Improvement   This refers to change which adds benefit or value to what the company already does. Basically, these changes build on existing procedures and activities rather than challenge them. They enhance or correct previously made policies and procedures. Staff are likely to feel threatened by this kind of change, but are readily able to understand the reasons for it when they are explained. *Examples*: the decision to upgrade equipment for increased return on investment, initiatives to decrease staff turnover or absenteeism, or quality programmes aimed to address customer complaints.

Innovative   This kind of change profoundly alters the way in which the company does business. It requires staff to rethink the way in which they behave and to alter long-standing work patterns. These changes are usually designed to address future company needs and potential problems rather than immediate ones. Staff, for that reason, may not understand their purpose and may resist accepting them for that reason. *Examples*: computerization for a paper-free office, robotics for precision manufacturing, satellite technology for global communication, or the move from line management to a project team model.

Requirements   It is very helpful to recognize what kind of change is required because each kind needs a different strategy. Managers aiming to *innovate* should be aware that resistance to this kind of change is likely to be much higher than for either *improvement* or *routine* change. The methods used for communication, leadership and activity coordination should be adapted to meet the varying needs of each change category.

Even a welcome innovation is often accompanied by some disruption to employees' lives with associated feelings of threatened security. There is a world of difference between telling line operators that they will be assembling an entirely new product line as opposed to their alternating from winter seasonal lines to the company's spring products. Managing innovative change requires use of different skills than managing routine change.

Analysing kinds of change   Often an analysis of the desired end result for change reveals which kind is required. Otherwise, the following questions help to decide the kind of change. The answers indicate what *kind* of change it is. Answers of 'yes' to the first three questions mean that it is a routine change. 'Yes' to questions four and five indicates an improvement change, and 'yes' to six and seven means innovation.

Routine
1 Is the change cyclical?
2 Do employees anticipate this change?
3 Does the change mean moving from one routine to another?

Improvement
4 Will the change provide a better way to conduct present activities?
5 Does change enhance an existing activity?

Innovative

6 Is the change an entirely new approach or idea for the company?
7 Does change require rethinking current company procedures?

Analysing company needs in terms of the three categories of routine, innovative and improvement is a first step to planning change. Once the kind of change is recognized, this influences all plans which relate to it. For example, innovative change takes up to five times as long as routine change to implement fully. This time is needed for training and encouraging staff, as well as for monitoring trial runs, dealing with delays and conducting in-depth evaluations.

Activity 2   *The three kinds of change have varying degrees of impact on staff and flow of work. This activity highlights these differences.*

Please think of three examples from your personal experience which illustrate each kind of change: routine, improvement, and innovative.

Column 1 in the following chart shows four ways in which change can have an impact. Each of your three examples of change should be given a score from 1 to 5, according to the degree of impact it had on these four items. Referring to your example, place this score in the appropriate column for routine, improvement or innovative change. A score of 5 shows a high degree of impact and a score of 1 shows a low degree.

Impact	Kinds of change		
	Routine	*Improvement*	*Innovative*
Amount of time to achieve			
Amount of disruption to flow of work			
Extent of training needs			
Amount of management time needed			

Table 1.1   Degrees of impact

Generally, routine changes have the lowest scores and innovative the highest. Improvement changes often vary according to how much they build on existing activities or emphasize new ideas. This matrix can also be used to determine the kind of change. For example, if a proposed idea can be achieved with low effort overall, it is likely to be a routine change, even if it looks highly innovative. It is always useful to consider the degree of disruption before launching any change effort.

Goals for change

Setting clear goals and deadlines provides a framework within which change can be achieved. When a plant manager is given a general directive such as, 'Establish safety measures to meet new regulatory standards', there are a range of complex issues to be considered which are associated with meeting 'new regulatory standards'. For example, there are potential labour problems if safety codes affect the organization of shift-work. There are possible hidden costs for training and equipment purchase which may cause the plant to run over budget. Where new or upgraded equipment must be ordered, then this capital expense affects the plant's return on investment figures and possibly the bonuses of individual managers. The list of related issues goes on and on.

Complicated change efforts require careful goal-setting. Some managers argue that going after a specific goal limits their ability to respond to events as they occur. In fact, goal-setting clarifies the needs of the situation and increases the accuracy of this response. Managers who understand all the necessary requirements have greater flexibility in managing change, not less. Clear goals provide direction and guide decisions about what must be done. Planning to achieve specific goals minimizes wasted time and effort.

It should be added that it is essential to recognize that the goals identified at this initial stage are open to revision, discussion and further fact-finding later. Managers of change are like explorers in unknown territory. They must scout terrain without maps and suffer lack of guarantee against accident or delay. Their first challenge is to clarify in precise terms where they want to go. As they proceed, they gradually discover vital information about the territory which leads to revision of their initial choice of goal.

A goal for change takes the form of a statement which is specific and positive. This is easier to suggest than to do, and can require several attempts in order to get it right. To return to the example of meeting new safety regulations, a first attempt could look like this:

'We need to change so that we can meet the new safety regulations.'

This simply repeats the general directive from the company's headquarters. A second try could include the awareness of some difficult issues which are involved in creating this change.

'We aim to change present safety standards so that they meet new regulations. Previous budget decisions must be evaluated in terms of added costs and possible

operational down-time. Understandings must be reached between management and labour about mutual benefits.'

By taking into account those business areas affected by the change, the manager outlines the next steps and makes explicit the company's priorities. After revising each goal statement, a manager should again ask, 'Does this statement refer to all the potential effects of the change?'

Activity 3   *This activity requires thinking of a current change initiative within your own organization. It highlights the need to refine goals for change. Please answer the following questions in terms of your own goal.*

1 Please think of an example of a goal for change.
2 What kind of goal is it? (routine, improvement, innovative)
3 Can it be expressed in more positive terms?
4 Can it be more specific?
5 Please refine your goal statement if necessary.

Five business areas   Focusing on several business areas at once is a challenging task and yet it ensures the creation of comprehensive goals. To make this task easier, it helps to cluster business activity into five general areas. This leads to considering the current state of the company systematically, area by area. The five business areas are:

- People
- Products and services
- Finance
- Facilities
- Marketing.

Initially any goal for change seems to have a greater impact on one area than on the others. In fact, the five areas are so interrelated and dependent upon each other that it is impossible not to influence them all by making an adjustment to one of them. Once a working goal for change is defined, then its potential impact on the other four areas can be assessed. By examining each area in turn, the associated effects become obvious. This effort leads to the refinement of the goal and of plans so that they benefit the whole of a company, not just an isolated part. It also prevents, or at least minimizes, the planning of any change which benefits one company division while contradicting the aims of another. The five business areas form a loop of interdependence:

People
This area refers to human resources in general as well as to administrative and management systems. Examples are: labour and management relations, decision-making process, hiring and firing procedures, salary and benefits issues, training, leadership styles, communication within the company, and many other issues.

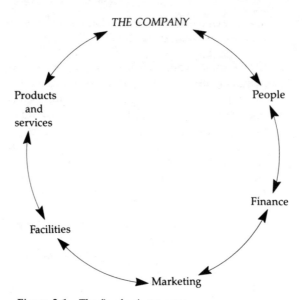

Figure 2.1   *The five business areas*

Products and services
This area refers to the nature of the company's business. First, there is a category of activity within which the company functions: from service industry, manufacturing, education, government, health, the professions, etc. Second, within the category, there are actual units of activity which the company produces: from material goods to a contracted service, and others.

Finance
This area refers to a company's financial position, its assets and liabilities, as well as to the control system within which these are organized. Decisions about finance must take into account both the long- and short-term needs of the company, balancing investment with expense toward the company's long-term viability.

Facilities
This area refers to the company's geographical situation, its physical environment (internal and external), as well as its equipment, electronic networks, and machinery. This highly sensitive area is most often ignored when planning change. This is to the company's peril. For example, the decision to remove a set of swing doors in order to improve access to machinery can also affect room temperature, increase noise levels or complicate work-flow and assembly. Another example: the purchase of upgrade equipment has a major impact on service capability as well as affecting year-end profits.

Marketing
This area refers to efforts which promote the company: its image and position within the industry. All of this affects the reactions of the audience which the company wishes to attract. Appropriate marketing measures directly contribute to the company's ability to attract and maintain business.

When all five areas are considered in turn and then in relation to each other, then the initially decided goal for change may seem less appropriate. For example, a manufacturer may decide to cut costs by delivering its own goods rather than using contracted freight services. This decision has an obvious effect on immediate costs, but it also has an impact upon staffing, insurance, capital expense and tax issues, to name but a few. Because this choice can influence the whole organization, a company should consider several available options for cutting costs before setting the objective of delivering its own goods. Evaluating the impact which this goal has on the whole company leads to its refinement or revision.

A systematic way to examine any goal for change is to gather all the available information about it and organize this data. This approach leads to a more informed decision as elements of risk emerge through examining each business area thoroughly. This was the course of action taken by Ian Halliday in this chapter's Prudential Assurance example.

It was also the intended course of the world-sector president in the cautionary tale of Chapter 1 (see page 6). Unfortunately, he gave his panel an overly simplified task. He then accepted the panel's evaluation as the single source of information for refining the company's goals for change. The president's initial goal for change was to relieve cash-flow pressures urgently. If he had referred to the five business areas, he would have recognized that any cash-oriented change would most obviously affect company finance. It would also influence the company's products because additional investment would be freed for needed research. The improved cash position would further allow greater pricing flexibility and potential increase in market share.

Although the least obvious areas of impact would be on people and facilities, a brief goal analysis would reveal that problems would most likely emerge from these sources. Having worked in the company himself for over 30 years, this president would have known that a change to facilities in this particular company would also mean changes to power base and managers' prestige. He would also realize that its management tradition routinely includes intimidation and blackmail. These realizations would lead to greater caution in selecting members for the panel and in depending upon it as a sole source of evaluation. This caution would have been warranted. The original, 'unrevised' report recommended dramatic reorganization of facilities and restructuring of the executive hierarchy.

A brief examination of a cash-oriented goal for change would reveal that every member of the panel would be potentially threatened by it. In retrospect, it is hard to believe that the president didn't predict what would happen. The fact is that he didn't, just as many managers of considerable competence and experience do not. This temporary lapse in judgement makes a strong case for even the most highly skilled managers to plan for change. Those goals which are chosen with awareness of their potential impact on the whole organization have most chance of contributing to its overall and long-term success.

Activity 4 *Please refer to the goal which you refined in Activity 3 (page 19). Answer the following questions in terms of this goal.*

1 Is this goal likely to disrupt one area of the company more than another? If so, how?
2 Does it contradict any other company initiatives or expressed company values? If so, how?
3 Can the goal be refined to include these additional points?

Five external forces The five business areas refer primarily to internal company activities. There are also five external forces which affect the company from the outside environment. Each of these areas should also be considered when setting goals for change. They are:

- Government
- Social values
- Technology
- Consumer need
- Competition.

These forces are influences which surround the company and have an impact on its business. While the company has control over the five internal areas, it has little, if any, control over the five forces surrounding it. The task of planning change includes studying and understanding outside

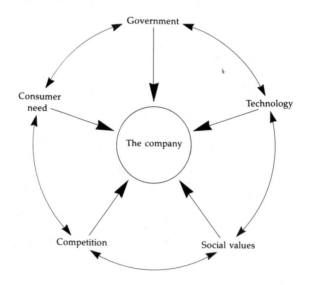

Figure 2.2 *The five external forces*

events in order to maximize benefit and minimize difficulty resulting from their influence. The five forces often have subtle effects on the company. They are interdependent and influence the company in complex ways.

Government

This area includes all political activity from legitimate as well as illegitimate authority. New legislation and terrorist activity can equally affect the company. Managers should consider past, present and possible future regulations, procedural codes, taxes and interest rates when deciding any goals for change.

Social values

This area includes health, education, morals, ethics, and social class issues. Awareness of current values is essential when evaluating benefits of any company change: from pollutant-free manufacturing practices to product development of low-cost medicine.

Technology

This area offers great risk and great benefit. The company which adapts to new methods may cut costs and capture new markets, but, there are also risks of over-investment in equipment with no guarantee of any gain. Managers must identify current improvement needs and long-term innovative measures.

Consumer need

This area refers to the company's customers: who they are, what they want and where they are located. Goals for change should include information gathered about customers both current and potential, demographic changes and fashion trends.

Competition

This area requires managers to be thoroughly aware of initiatives and developments within their industry. Competition provides alternatives to consumers. Any change should reinforce the customers' demand for the company's own products.

The forces from the external environment add another dimension to evaluating goals for change. Their impact is extremely difficult to estimate, but it is essential to meet this challenge. Otherwise, plans for change may lack vital features which would ensure the change initiative's success.

Activity 5   *Please refer to the goal you developed and refined in Activities 3 and 4 (pages 19 and 22). Answer the following questions in terms of this goal.*

1 Does this goal create any opportunities from outside the company?
2 Could this goal lead to any threats from outside the company?
3 If so, how can the goal be refined to respond to these points?

What needs evaluation

It can seem premature to think about evaluating change before either planning or implementing it. Even so, it is useful to do so at the beginning of the project because this guides decisions about data collection and how success will be measured at the project's end. Much time is wasted and information lost if managers wait until completion of the change to decide what information they need in order to measure success.

For example, if statistical measures are required at intervals during the change, this must be decided in advance. Also, the timing of the intervals should be planned and the basis for the measurements determined. Waiting until the end of the project to decide these issues means increased effort. It is equally awkward to discover that 'before' and 'after' interviews are needed to document successful change. At the project's end, participants can never return to their 'before' state. The information is essentially lost.

Those outside a project can believe even a successful change has been poorly executed when evaluation methods are not organized or are incomplete. Each evaluation requirement should be outlined at the beginning of the change when the goals are identified. In addition, a specific deadline should be given for collecting this information. If interim reports are needed, those implementing the change need to know all scheduling requirements. This is the kind of detail that is most often missed.

Suggested methods

Interviews
This consists of a set of questions for individuals or groups. The specific questions should be decided in advance if 'before' and 'after' interviews are required. Alternatively, if completion interviews *only* are needed, general categories for the questions can be decided in advance and then revised as necessary when the project ends.

Behaviour observation
If the change aims to encourage different behaviour or impart new skills, then these should be listed. Ask: 'What specifically should be observed?' If the change led to unexpected behaviour, the initial list of desired results can be compared to the actual observations.

Statistical measures
This method requires that the sample size and product specifications should be decided in advance. These affect any plans for data collection. Criteria for choosing the specifications and calculation figures must be documented. The rationale for the tests should not depend on memory or the skill of single individuals.

Anonymous surveys
Chapter 5 provides detailed instructions for producing individualized questionnaires and surveys. At the beginning of a project, it should be decided what information is needed from participants and how it will be obtained.

Time studies

This method is related to observation of the time that is required to complete tasks. Logistics can be complex, and so decisions about what and who should be studied must be incorporated into plans.

Quality inspection

This requires defining what quality means in relation to the change, and then deciding what system will be used to measure that the goals for quality are actually met. This can depend on specialized product needs or quality control standards in the company.

Other methods

Each project has unique and specialized needs which should be considered when planning change.

Activity 6   *Please refer to the goal you developed in Activity 5 (page 23). Answer the following questions in terms of this goal.*

1 What evaluation methods do you intend using to measure the success of this change?
   - interviews
   - behaviour observation
   - statistical measures
   - anonymous surveys
   - time studies
   - quality inspection
   - other methods
2 How frequently should evaluation occur?
3 Is there a deadline for the change to be achieved?
4 Are there mid-project goals to be achieved? If so, what are their deadlines?
5 If the mid-project goals are not achieved, how will you decide whether plans for change need adjustment?

Problem— analysis— discussion

Problem   A computer hardware manufacturer moves to new facilities which provide 300 workstation spaces for a sales staff of 350 employees. Simultaneously, the company invites its staff to work from their homes on a regular basis. The management promotes this measure as a benefit for their trusted staff. Unfortunately, the staff do not believe this and associate the new move and work-at-home invitation as part of a cost-cutting initiative.

The workstations are available on a first-come-first-served basis and managers are treated to the sight of their sales staff arriving earlier and earlier every day. Within three months of the move, sales figures have dropped and the sales department atmosphere has deteriorated as members argue over access to clerical support and office equipment. The managing director, the financial controller and the sales manager meet to identify what changes should now be made. Among their ideas are:

1 Return to the old system of one desk for each staff member.
2 Initiate a team-building effort to encourage sharing and cooperation.
3 Provide pay incentives so that employees can offset costs of working at home (increased heat, light, phone).

These managers acknowledge among themselves that it was a mistake to represent the work-at-home suggestion as a staff benefit rather than a cost-cutting measure. While their initial decision arose from financial need, they are now faced with human needs, apparent shortage of facilities and a negative impact on their markets. They realize that making a major company decision with a limited perception of the whole situation was unwise and costly, but this awareness doesn't help them to resolve the situation.

Analysis   *Take a moment to imagine yourself in the predicament of these managers. The following questions help to organize the available information.*

1 What kind of change was this initially?
  Routine   Innovative   Improvement
2 What kind of change has it become?
  Routine   Innovative   Improvement
3 Identify the current need for change. Include reference to the five internal and five external features in the goal statement.
4 How will you evaluate further change to determine whether it is successful?

Discussion   Although the management team originally planned to innovate, their present situation requires that they improve their initial plan for change. Improvement change is normally less difficult to implement. In this case, the innovation has created so much confusion and mistrust that any correction must prove time-consuming. It would be best if the management team explores the need for change as if no action had yet been taken. This would give them necessary insight to improve their current situation.

First, they should examine again the merits of removing 50 workstations. In this case, the management team knows that, on any one day, there are less than 280 sales representatives at workstations. In addition, these staff are rarely in the office for an entire working day. Actual sales work is conducted outside the office while visiting clients and prospective customers.

These data allow the management team to reaffirm their goal of 'reducing workstations from 350 to 300 in the new premises.' But they also need to examine the five business areas in order to refine this goal. With the benefit of hindsight, their analysis produces this result.

Finance
The change to facilities reduces company overheads while burdening some staff with operating costs. We need more information about the extent of these costs, but believe that the company should offset them.

Marketing
Because the change has affected sales through confusion and poor follow-up from representatives, our goal should now include a reference to maintaining projected sales figures throughout the change.

Products and services
Although the change intended to improve customer service, it has had the reverse effect. Our goal should include the provision of increased efficiency for customer service.

People
We now realize that this is the weakest area of our plan. It is counter-productive to manipulate the truth with highly knowledgeable staff. When we told staff that the change was a new staff benefit and denied its relation to cost-cutting, we lost credibility. Further communication should offer honest, clear information with an explanation of the thinking behind the change.

To identify what staff need in order to make the change work, we tried putting ourselves in their place. This led us to discover that there is now inadequate office support for conducting company business. The previous office was arranged so that staff worked in clusters, sharing equipment, the time of clerical staff, and office space. The new arrangement makes no provision for these work habits and also offers no substitute for arranging flexible clerical support.

Although clerical staff are still available, they are now organized into a pool, rather than assigned to separate units. Problems arise when sales staff fax the office for vital information and receive no reply. Even urgent requests are often ignored. The attention of support staff is absorbed by those who are physically in the office. This, more than the desire for a private desk, leads to the early arrivals in the office and the competition for equipment.

Having recognized that the innovation does not take into account the special needs of the sales staff, we are now asking for suggestions from them about improving office organization. Feedback is also to be solicited from clerical and other support staff to create a new system.

Facilities
This area needs a thorough examination. Along with the people-related issues, equipment and office furniture will have to be organized to meet the employees' needs.

The revised goal for change becomes:

The company's move to new premises allows the reduction of workstations from 350 to 300. This increases efficiency and reduces overheads. Sales staff can choose to work from home at company expense, with office support organized to make this possible. During transition to the new arrangement, projected sales figures are to be maintained.

Summary

When identifying specific goals for change, it is more important to be accurate than fast. Care should be exercised to gather as much information as is possible from every available source. Change based on the perceptions of a single company leader leaves much to chance. When the views of many experienced people are included, then the change initiative is more likely to succeed.

There are three kinds of change: routine, improvement, and innovative. Recognizing the kind of change allows a manager to plan an appropriate strategy. Each kind requires different degrees of preparation. Goals for change must be specific. Managers should consider five business areas when planning change. These are: products and services, people, markets, facilities, and finance. They should also be aware of five external forces. These are government, social values, technology, consumer need, and competition.

A clearly defined goal for change allows a manager to plan how to evaluate success when the project is complete. Decisions about data collection for final project evaluation should be made at the beginning of the project, rather than at the end.

Selected reading

Argenti, John, *Practical Corporate Planning* (rev. ed.). London: Unwin Hyman, 1989.

Barnett, John H. and Wilsted, William D., *Strategic Management: Text and Concepts.* Boston: PWS-Kent Publishing, 1989.

Croon, Peter, *Strategy and Strategy Creation.* Rotterdam: Rotterdam University Press, 1974.

London, Manuel, *Change Agents: New Roles and Innovation Strategies for Human Resource Professionals.* San Francisco: Jossey-Bass, 1988.

Pearce, John A. II and Robinson, Richard B. Jr., *Corporate Stategies: A Selection of Readings from Business Week.* New York: McGraw-Hill, 1986.

Porter, Michael, *Competitive Advantage: Creating and Sustaining Superior Performance.* New York: The Free Press, 1985.

3 Considering company context

A wider perspective

It is inevitable that past and present events influence the future. When planning change, it makes sense to look at the whole life-span of the company before committing to any new initiatives. This means examining company history, resources, its position in the market place, vision and patterns of company growth, among other issues. The previous chapter discussed the setting of clear goals. This chapter emphasizes that these goals should also contribute to the needs of the company as a whole, not just enhance one of its parts, divisions or departments.

Initiating an isolated change without considering the larger company context is a high-risk proposition. Projects which are based on a narrow examination of company needs can offer limited benefit or create confusion and contradict other company initiatives. A strategic approach aligns every goal for change with the larger company vision. These goals are coordinated so that costly duplication of effort and adverse effects of internal company competition are avoided.

This means that managers must understand the needs of the company as a whole and define goals for change with these in mind. Studying the company's larger context is the second stage in the four-stage method for managing change. It is an important part of the process because it leads to an improved understanding of what needs to change. Time spent on this is well invested because this in-depth company knowledge can be drawn upon again and again when managing future changes.

Even company founders who believe they know every aspect of their firms can benefit from this process. It allows them to assume the role of impartial observer when they examine their company. As an 'outsider', they can look at its activities with a fresh perspective and ask with as much objectivity as is possible: 'What does this situation need?' Any new insight leads to reconsidering the goals for change and deciding whether they truly add to or detract from the company as a whole.

The skill of shifting attention from the specific needs of an isolated part of the company to include the more global needs of the whole is a basic one for managers of change and is the foundation of strategic thinking. Unfortunately, the ability to change or shift perspective can create difficulties for individual leaders. They can feel a conflict of loyalties if they discover that a change benefiting their own work teams must be delayed or even suspended when it is assessed in terms of company

need. Such are the challenges of analysis. Although additional information creates complications, the decisions for change which are finally
made are wiser and provide greater satisfaction. Ultimately, good
decisions benefit everyone.

This chapter emphasizes the importance of setting goals for change that
enhance the whole company. Four questions are posed to guide the
analysis of company context. They serve to increase an understanding of
precisely what changes should occur. These questions are:

1 What is unique, special and different about this company?
2 What is the company's market edge?
3 Is there an overall strategy for growth?
4 Does the goal match company needs?

Case study

Kern Konsult

> **The purpose of this case study is to illustrate the importance of
> recognizing company values and goals before initiating a programme
> for change. The manager involved describes unforeseen difficulties
> which arose from company expansion. He also outlines the steps he
> took to resolve the problems from this initial change.**

Kern Konsult is a professional firm based in Bussum near Amsterdam
with an exceptional reputation for management development, quality
programmes and project management. Daniel Ofman, co-founder and
managing director, believes their success results from a commitment to
serve the good of society as well as the encouragement of staff to
develop professionally and personally.

Ironically, idealism and inspiring standards can create discomfort, confusion
and even pain before they lead to beneficial and profitable growth. Daniel
says, ' "Kern" means "core" in English, and this refers to our core values.
The more people are involved in policy-making and company direction,
the more they need to know where their ideas originate. Are they based
on ambition, dreams, egotism, greed? Are they an expression of what
this company is supposed to be?' He emphasizes the importance of
these issues at Kern Konsult as he describes a major change which
actually undermined the values on which the company was founded.

Five years ago, the company consisted of Daniel, his partner, Willem
Renes, and support staff. The two partners decided to expand, and so
they recruited more consultants. One of these showed obvious partner
potential. During the following year, two others also joined. Because it
felt appropriate for them to become partners, Willem and Daniel
decided that all three new members should be given shares and be
made partners. Soon after this, they accepted a fourth new partner.

Daniel says, 'In just six months, we went from two partners to six. Idealism made us do this. We gave everyone equal shares because we didn't want there to be different levels in the company: senior and junior. This was ridiculous because we were different. All of our business and the concepts we used were generated and developed by Willem and myself.'

During the next year, Daniel gradually discovered that the rapid increase of partners as well as the hiring of additional consultants brought unexpected problems. 'I had known these four men for many years and believed that we shared the same values. Though I still have high respect for them all, I am now aware that there were questions which I didn't ask. I had no clear understanding of the differences between us.' In general terms, the four agreed to the policies and values of the company. In specifics, they wanted to change these in ways which Daniel believed would completely alter the integrity and innovative nature of the company.

Three major issues emerged during the first year of the new partnership: (a) the four resisted giving to charity (it was a Kern Konsult policy to give one-third of its profits to charitable organizations); (b) the four gave priority to conventional commercial objectives (Kern Konsult emphasized business success through personal clarity and self-awareness); and (c) the four wanted to produce a brochure which highlighted the six partners (Kern Konsult in the past avoided splitting partners from staff, as 'us' versus 'them').

Daniel described the difficulty the six partners had in resolving these differences. 'We had no process for resolving conflict and discussing the shadowy side of our personalities. I was always the one questioning what we were doing and so got the label of 'trouble-maker'. Because I was meeting chairman, our discussions got grimmer and grimmer.'

After numerous attempts to resolve their problems, Daniel finally decided that he should leave the firm. Daniel explains, 'There is one area where I don't make compromises and that is in the area of values.' Just as he reached this conclusion, Willem visited him at his home and suggested that they leave Kern Konsult together and start all over again. 'It only took a minute for me to agree. When we told our four partners, they couldn't believe us. The real surprise came from the staff and all the associate consultants. When it was announced that we would leave, they met and decided that they wanted to leave with us. For the first time, the four *had to look* at themselves. In the end it was they who decided to leave the company.'

In summation, there were three phases to Kern Konsult's expansion programme. First, there was a phase of rapid growth: the addition of four partners and additional consultants. This created a sudden alteration of the company's context, its values and even the reason for its existence. Second, this led the two founding partners to regret the choices that they had made. They took action to adjust this by announcing that they would leave the firm. In fact, they stayed with Kern Konsult and the four partners chose to leave.

Finally, Daniel and Willem created a third phase after the four partners left. They established a clear financial policy with profit-sharing and regular donations to charity, a process for developing their employees' talents and skills, and an explicit statement of their company's values. Daniel adds, 'The discussion about commitment to values is now integrated into our bi-monthly business meetings. It is extremely important. We ask our staff to give feedback about how we are all living up to our stated beliefs.'

To sum up, he says, 'Change is a searching process. I don't know any better way of dealing with it than to be receptive, alert and available all the time to discover what really needs to change. Going through this process was very painful and very important. Without it, I would not be where I am now in terms of my work with clients and my ability to run this company.'

What is unique, special and different?

To answer this question it is necessary to first look at the company's basic strengths: those which make the company unique, special and different and which account for its position in the market place. When setting goals for change this information is critically important. Because any change which inadvertently alters or negatively affects a basic company strength actually creates double trouble: first, because it fails to address the original need for change, and second, because it undermines at least one source of the company's advantage over the competition. In the case of Kern Konsult, Daniel Ofman had the necessary courage and management skill to create a successful outcome from serious difficulties. None of this was easy for him, either personally or professionally.

Ambitious managers should be warned: no one will thank them for saving time, if an end result leads to the loss of either customers or an advantage over the competition. The educated guess and seat-of-the-pants school of change management produces successful results primarily in folklore and the biographies of industrial leaders. In reality, an exhaustive understanding of a company's strengths and what distinguishes it from its competition leads to change which has a chance of success. Leaders who take a strategic approach use their knowledge of the company to contribute further to developing a market edge over their competition.

This market edge is sometimes referred to as *distinctive competence*. This means an *important company strength* which *satisfies a demand in the market place* and which also *provides the company with an advantage over the competition*.

Consider the hypothetical example of an entrepreneur in the mid-eighties who decides to compete with the major international companies in the sale of computers. He sees these major firms spending millions to promote the advantages of personal computer use at home, but their equipment is priced far too high for the average family. The entrepreneur realizes that similar 'clone' equipment could be produced far more cheaply, and so he sets out to do this.

As a clone computer manufacturer, he pioneers the sale of inexpensive, quality equipment which is fully compatible with the market leaders. His declared *market edge* is defined as 'lower price with equal quality and compatibility.' This statement signifies much more than a company slogan. It describes a *customer demand* for equal quality and compatibility. It also highlights a *specific advantage* over the competition, that is, lower price.

In response, the competition could choose to lower their prices to match the clone company. If this happens, the entrepreneur must seriously consider what other competitive advantage his company can promote. Perhaps he could provide high quality local service or on-site training schemes. He would then revise his market edge definition to: equal quality and compatibility with unbeatable service or with personalized training schemes.

When defining market edge, the company's five business areas and five external forces should be considered. Because these factors change with time, market edge should be evaluated regularly to include new situations and events. Recognizing those strengths which satisfy a demand and also beat the competition is a vitally important management exercise. All major change initiatives should be developed so that they contribute to market edge.

Diversified companies

In very large and heavily diversified companies, discovering market edge offers an added challenge. One response is to define diversity as one feature of market edge. This idea falls down if the company's major competitors are equally diversified. When defining market edge, the task is to put aside conventionally accepted beliefs about the company's source of success. Instead, begin at the beginning. Ask: what makes this company as a whole unique, special and different? Then, what makes its separate divisions unique, special and different?

From the overall collection of company resources and strengths a collage of answers is created. Many factors which contribute to market edge emerge in the process. Each of these should be evaluated toward defining what the company as a whole does best in terms of customer demand and competitive advantage. A clear understanding of what the company aims to achieve in the market place leads to decisions which make change easier to plan and then to implement.

Departmental or divisional change

When company leaders clarify market edge, this influences change and development throughout the company. In the example of the clone computer company, a major strength is provision of quality equipment. When this message is communicated throughout the company, division supervisors can plan any major change in production, research, marketing and other areas so that it contributes to the market edge. When purchasing supplies, for example, managers would choose to minimize costs but also avoid purchase of inferior materials. Plans would then include larger volume purchases, building long-term relationships with suppliers, or improving inventory control, but never short-term saving from use of poor quality goods.

When planning training initiatives, quality would be emphasized as a company principle. New managers would be encouraged to make decisions which enhance the company's published market edge. This enables them to take action with greater confidence because they have the benefit of clear guidelines from the top of the company.

What is the market edge?

Making an inventory of the company's resources is a good place to begin defining company strengths. This should only include current resources, not potential ones or those which were available in the past. This may seem an obvious point. Unfortunately, an absolute belief in a proposal or even an emotional tie to the past can undermine any manager's ability to consider new ideas with necessary clarity and objectivity.

For example, if a proposed change includes the purchase of a distribution centre in a key geographical location, this centre cannot be listed as a current resource. Including it assumes the benefit of ownership and makes an analysis of the current resources meaningless. A thorough review of resources should come before examination of the proposal to purchase the centre. The review can then reveal alternatives to the purchase if they are available.

Alternatively, if the distribution centre is no longer a resource through sale or other loss, then all features associated with it must be excluded from a list of company resources. Those managers who have taken for granted the centre's benefits in the past must make themselves fully aware of those specific features which are no longer available. These altered circumstances often reveal additional hidden costs in organizational time, lost suppliers' goodwill and slower delivery of goods. All of these must be taken into account when defining market edge.

Resources: tangible and intangible

A list of its assets provides an indicator of company resources. This list should also include the skills and attitudes of all employees, along with cash, equipment and facilities. Other assets which could be overlooked are relationships with customers, regulatory bodies, investors and suppliers. All of these features comprise resources: some tangible and some intangible.

The five business areas discussed in the previous chapter provide a means of organizing an inventory of company resources. Each area's features can also be separated into those which are tangible and those which are intangible. A partial list of resources which are typically available to companies is offered here.

Products and services

Tangible	*Intangible*
• ready supply of raw materials	• production flexibility (systems and methods)
• copyrights, patents	• strong research and development focus
• quality control programme	• quality assurance philosophy
• review of competition	• contacts within the industry (networks, allies, friends)

People

Tangible	*Intangible*
• training programmes	• technical expertise
• contracts and commitments	• leadership stability (on all levels)
• trained labour in long-term employment	• skilled labour is readily available
• employee grievance procedures	• emphasis on interpersonal skills
• effective communication systems	• creative input from all employee levels
• satisfactory fee, salary, benefits agreements	• labour–management cooperation

---

Finance

Tangible	*Intangible*
• control systems	• strong financial controller and accounts staff
• budget and update information at regular intervals	• financial goals explicit and agreed by those concerned
• adequate capital for short and long term	• financial planning and skilled advisers
• debt facility available as needed	• good relationship with investors and lenders

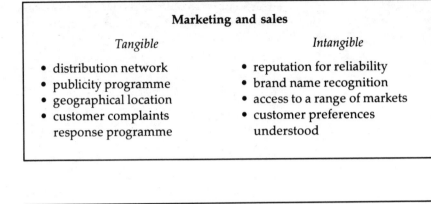

Marketing and sales

Tangible

- distribution network
- publicity programme
- geographical location
- customer complaints
  response programme

Intangible

- reputation for reliability
- brand name recognition
- access to a range of markets
- customer preferences
  understood

Facilities

Tangible

- modern technology:
  equipment, machinery
- adequate space, lighting
  and cleanliness
- janitorial and equipment
  maintenance arranged
- safety standards met

Intangible

- efficient use of time and
  materials
- attractive work environment

- efficiency and minimum
  down-time
- minimum liability and staff
  sense of security

Activity 7   *Part 1*

Please circle those business features from the preceding list of resources which you believe your company possesses. These circled resources form a partial list of your company's strengths. What other specific strengths does your company have? Expand your list to include these additional strengths. You can refer to the five external forces (see page 22) for other sources of strength.

Part 2

When assessing company strengths, bias and blind spots can create human error. A manager's perceptions can perpetuate the behaviour or mistakes of the past or limit the company's ability to innovate. It is entirely possible for managers to assume that a company feature is a strength when actually it is not. Before deciding that each of the listed strengths contributes positively to the company's marketing edge, a short survey is in order.

Please return to your circled company resources and the additional items listed in Part 1 of this activity.

1 Does this item directly contribute to customer demand? If so, write a 'D' next to it. If you are uncertain, write a question mark.

2 Does this item directly create an advantage over the competition? If so, write a 'C' next to it. If you are uncertain, put a question mark.
3 Make a list here of every item which both contributes to customer demand and adds an advantage over the competition.

If there are questions about whether just a few resources directly add to customer demand or to an advantage over the competition, these resources may enhance the company indirectly or in subtle ways. If there are questions or uncertainty about most items, then this indicates that the company must examine the demand for its products and redefine which customers it wishes to serve. After clarifying and articulating this, company resources and strengths can be more readily assessed in terms of demand and competition. With this information, market edge can be determined and plans for change can be developed which contribute to market edge rather than undermine it inadvertently.

Part 3

1 Make a list of all the resources to which you gave both a 'D' and a 'C'. Choose one from this list. Write in specific terms how this resource meets customer demand and how it gives an advantage over the competition.
2 Continue to do this for each item on the list.
3 Do any phrases or words come to mind which summarize how the company meets customer demand and competitive advantage?
4 What is your statement for market edge?

Defining market edge

When assessing the company for market edge, there is a sequence which should be followed. First, list all of its resources. Second, decide which of these are important company strengths. Third, analyse each strength to discover if it directly contributes to customer demand as well as provides a competitive advantage. Fourth, those strengths which both meet a demand and give an advantage are sources of market edge. Look these over to develop a statement which describes market edge. Figure 3.1 summarizes the definition process. Company leaders invest in success when they provide their colleagues with a clear statement of market edge.

Problem— analysis— discussion

Problem

The following problem highlights the importance of recognizing market edge.

The newly hired division director for a mail order company observed the sales telephonists conversing with customers as they took their orders. Most of these staff were female, and the director assumed that

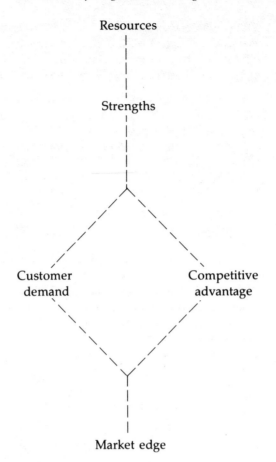

Figure 3.1 *Sequence for defining market edge*

they were enjoying a gossip at the company's expense. Although many of them were long-term employees, he also believed that they took too casual an attitude toward their high-pressure job. Three weeks later, the director received a routine request from the telephonists' supervisor to hire additional seasonal staff. On the strength of his initial impression, he refused to approve this.

Instead, he suggested that present staff levels should be used more efficiently. When the supervisor showed him the department's consistently high figures for telephone sales against industry averages, the director remained firm. He said, 'With greater efficiency, those figures will be even higher.' Unfortunately, the lower staff numbers during a season of record high orders affected the department's overall effectiveness as well as the morale of the telephonists. The amount of returned merchandise actually doubled compared with the previous year and for the first time in the company's history the mail order division showed no real growth of sales during the peak season.

Analysis   *Take a minute to imagine yourself in the role of this division director after just assuming your post. You have noticed the telephonists' behaviour and you also know the successful sales history for your division. Answer these questions as if you wish to improve efficiency in mail order sales.*

1 Assume that the telephonists' conversation with customers is an advantage. List three possible benefits of this behaviour to telephone sales.
2 Assume that their behaviour is a disadvantage. List three possible problems for the department.
3 What customer demand could the telephonists serve?
4 What possible advantage do they give the company over the competition?
5 What should be considered when setting a goal for improved efficiency in terms of (a) customer demand; (b) competitive advantage?

Discussion   In this example, the director perceived the telephonists' behaviour to be a weakness. He considered each sales call as an isolated incident and decided that the calls took a longer time than was necessary. When he chose to limit staff numbers during the peak season, he based this decision on a guess that efficiency was directly linked to the amount of time spent on each call. He imagined that shorter calls would lead to greater efficiency. He further believed that telephonists who developed work habits during 10 to 15 years' service would be able or willing abruptly to change their regular routine for handling customers.

This director would have been wiser to consider first the specific customer demand which the telephonists' behaviour satisfied, then question whether their behaviour gave the company any advantage over other mail order sales companies. To gather this information, he should have monitored the sales calls and actually listened to the substance of the conversations. He could also have interviewed several long-term staff for additional information.

He would have discovered that the telephonists took pride in their knowledge of the catalogue's merchandise. They advised customers when items were 'cut rather large' or 'ran small'. Their knowledge of the company's products led directly to the low percentage of returned goods. The conversational aspects of the sales calls were similar to the pleasantries and remarks from sales staff in quality retail shops.

Unfortunately, the director did not recognize any of this. By initiating change during a time of peak pressure, he strained the department's resources. Also, his manner of communicating the change undermined the telephonists' morale at a time when they needed most encouragement. All of this could have been avoided if he had been willing to question his own impressions. This director should have considered market edge before initiating a major change. He would have benefited from challenging his own biases and habits of mind.

Framing— reframing

The definition of framing as it appears in a standard dictionary is: 'an established order or system, or the way that a thing may be constructed, organized or formed'. Management trainers and business study specialists have adopted the term 'framing' for an educational purpose. They use it to refer to the habits of mind which individuals develop to view and interpret the world. Each person 'frames' experience according to the idiosyncratic logic of his or her own mind. These frames are highly individual and dependent on personal values, background and understanding. For example, two individuals seeing the same film may interpret it differently. Their interpretations emerge from the way in which they habitually think. This is their basic world view or frame of reference.

Framing is a useful concept when considering the company's larger context. When managers identify how they frame the company, they take a crucial step toward developing greater objectivity about company activities. Frames—or habits of mind—can create limits to accurate assessment of company strengths and to the ability to envision change. Recognizing the limitations of their mental frames leads managers to reconsider their own opinions and biases.

In the mail order company problem, the division director framed the telephonists' behaviour as inefficient and self-serving. This frame limited his ability to work effectively with his staff. Perhaps this was based on past experience with other telephone sales departments, or on gender bias. The telephonists were all women, the gender burdened with stereotypes of chattiness and a tendency to gossip. The main issue is not the *source* of the frame, rather the *limits* it placed on the director's ability to manage them and the change effectively.

Like any habit, framing is changeable, but it takes effort and the will to make this happen. Having identified how a situation is framed, it becomes possible to step back from it and then choose to 'reframe' it. That is, it is possible to make a conscious choice to interpret what is seen and heard in a different way than mental habit dictates. This means looking for the positives when normally there are only negatives or vice versa. Changing a frame requires asking what other meaning can be found in the observed events.

This self-questioning expands management potential. Successful change is undermined less by events than by company leaders' inability to imagine the right course of action. The discipline of framing and reframing leads to the flexible thinking needed to manage change.

Activity 8   *Part 1: Framing*

Take a moment to consider a current problem situation or person at work. This can be unrelated to a change effort or initiative. Please answer the following questions toward discovering how you frame the problem.

1 Briefly describe the problem.
2 How serious do you find this problem on a scale of 1 to 10 (1 = low and 10 = high)?
3 What are its most difficult or challenging features?
4 How long has this problem existed?
5 What is its most obvious or visible cause?

Part 2: Reframing

Now forget about the problem as you described it in Part 1. Consider instead your work environment as a whole, how your area of responsibility interacts with other areas and also how work projects merge with them. Please answer the following questions toward creating a reframe for your problem.

1 Briefly describe the larger context surrounding the problem.
2 How much does this larger context have an impact on the problem on a scale from 1 to 10 (1 = low and 10 = high)?
3 What aggravates the problem: events, people, procedures?
4 Is there any pattern to this aggravation?
5 Are there any hidden causes of the problem or unhealthy influences from this context?

Examine your answers in Part 2 toward discovering a different interpretation of the problem. Ask yourself, 'Is there any other meaning or emphasis which could be given to this situation?' It helps to forget the originally labelled problem situation or person, and consider the events, people or procedures with a fresh perspective. If this is too difficult, ask yourself, 'How would an outsider interpret this situation or these interactions and events?'

A reframe of the problem is based on *new insight*. Obvious alternative interpretations or beliefs which immediately come to mind are not likely to be reframes. The task is *discovery* of a new perspective. A reframe provides a completely new interpretation of events or behaviour. These new ideas are not necessarily correct, but the point of reframing is to challenge at every instance any tendency to narrow-minded thinking and single-idea mental habits. Managers of change need flexible thinking in order to understand their company's needs more clearly. Reframing broadens a manager's perspective.

To return to the mail order company director, a reframe for him would have been the realization that the telephonists were serious, conscientious and committed to their work. This characterization would have challenged his original view that they were 'taking advantage' of their company seniority. In this case, the reframe provided a more accurate interpretation of their work and could have led to a successful choice for change rather than a disastrous one.

Further practice Another practice exercise to develop these skills consists of reframing a highly negative colleague's behaviour. First, ask: How does this person's *negativity* contribute to the company? Among the answers could be included:

- provides a contrast to positive people
- polarizes some people with neutral feelings to be more positive
- provides a consistent source of information about problems
- provides an 'extreme' example which can be used whenever an illustration of negativity is needed
- establishes a base-line for reading company morale.

Reframing negative situations or people's behaviour allows positive features to emerge. This practice leads to 'immunity' from over-reaction to this negativity, however severe it seems. Developing a wider perspective creates greater choice. Rather than react to a complaint with a counter-attack, it becomes possible to consider what merit, if any, it contains. Reframing is one of the best available methods for maintaining a sense of humour and a calm attitude during difficult moments. This in itself is a powerful intervention when managing change.

What is the growth strategy?

Answering this question requires an analysis of company history, particularly those past events which contribute most to its present development. Often, there is a lack of documentation about growth decisions or the intentions of former company leaders. Determined managers can study the historical results of those decisions, though, toward better understanding how the company has become what it is. They can discover what patterns there are, if any, to the way the company has grown.

Just as frames limit individuals, rigid patterns of growth can constrict a company's ability to innovate and develop as needed. Identifying the presence of patterns leads to decisions among company leaders about whether to continue with them. For middle managers, recognizing these patterns allows them to manage change so that they cooperate with 'the way things are done in the company'. For example, predatory management behaviour is not rewarded in a company which has traditionally employed a growth strategy based on cooperation among allies outside the company and on team work within.

Company growth strategy is the product of its leaders' temperaments and the accumulation over time of the procedures they create. It is one aspect of 'corporate culture', a term which frequently appears in business literature today. Culture, in this sense, is the accumulation of habits and procedures, management and decision-making style, and the company atmosphere in general. This results from company history, patterns of growth, and leaders' preferences. A single, individual leader cannot change a company's culture or even adjust it without tremendous effort of will. Even a team of leaders cannot make decisions about company culture without having to address the momentum created by the decisions of their predecessors.

Although company resources, strengths and market edge add to the understanding of company culture, another essential factor is the pattern of growth. This section describes four basic growth strategies. These four actually represent many related strategies clustered into general categories for easier analysis, and are: concentrated effort, internal growth, acquisition, and disinvestment. The way the company has expanded in the past and how it interacts with other companies can be indicators of its growth strategy.

It can be argued that a company has many growth strategies, depending on its developmental stage. More often, companies show 'habits' of growth, that is, an underlying style for expansion which recurs through-out the company's history. These patterns in many cases result from either the conscious preferences or unconscious drives of company leaders.

Given the number of mergers, de-mergers, company closures and employee buy-outs during the last few years, it may not be possible to determine a pattern of growth. This section is an aid for managers who can draw on basic information about the company. The way that the company tends to grow is one more piece of information to help manage change more effectively.

Four strategies

Concentrated effort

The company which adopts this strategy emphasizes a single product or service. If there is more than one, the company products are interrelated and thoroughly integrated into the business. This would be the manu-facturing firm which specializes in a single product, such as the distillers of single malt whiskys. It is also the professional firm which offers a specialized service, such as legal advice for the building industry.

Growth from a strategy of concentration most often depends on gaining market share from competitors or applying new research to improve the current product line, thereby increasing sales. An example of this strategy is the wax-coated paper manufacturer which maintained a commitment to its product in spite of severe competition during the 'seventies from plastic wraps and aluminium foil manufacturers. With the advent of microwave ovens in the 'eighties, waxed paper regained its popularity and this one-product strategy finally paid off.

Concentration is a low-risk strategy as long as there is a market for the product. Managers of change in this environment should recognize the limitations of this strategy as well as its strengths. When proposing alterations to a single product line or suggesting a radical change to this product, managers should be prepared for resistance. New ideas need detailed explanation and an excellent rationale. Company leaders are not necessarily conservative; they simply believe in their product, although, on occasion, resistance is due to lack of ambition or capital. Managers can cooperate with a concentration strategy by presenting ideas for change in terms of their enhancement of the present product line.

Internal growth

The company which adopts this strategy gradually adds new products and services to its existing line in order to adapt to changing fashions and tastes. An example would be the manufacturer of men's electric shavers which identifies a demand from women for a similar product. With altered packaging, the company is able to sell the same product to a completely new market. Another type of internal growth strategy is illustrated by the company which realizes that one of their main products is becoming obsolete. Gradually, they substitute different but similar products. During the 'sixties, manufacturers of the popular transistor radio maintained growth and long-term success by developing other electronic goods as complements to a fad item.

As the need for one item vanishes, the strategy is to guide the company into production of a related product. This is another low-risk strategy. Success depends on the ability to identify appropriate new and complementary products based on the company's existing strengths.

The internal environment in a company with this strategy is likely to be highly competitive. New ideas from employees would be sought and used. Reward and advancement would depend on company leaders' style and tendencies. Managers of change in such companies should describe their ideas in terms of how they contribute to the long-term viability of the company rather than the success of a specific product. They should promote their own successful activities. This is a necessary step in very competitive environments.

Acquisition

This strategy emphasizes growth through acquiring other companies, and there can be several leadership motivations for this tactic. One of these is the acquisition of companies which provide similar goods and services to those of the purchasing company; for example, a beer producer buys out all the local competitors. Buy-out is an aggressive way to deal with the competition, but the motivation can be varied: from price control to empire building to revenge to many alternatives.

A purchasing company can also seek to acquire the suppliers of its raw materials or needed resources. In this case, this can be a defensive strategy ensuring that the company maintains a source of necessary supply or the ability to market its products. For example, the owners of oil fields may seek control of refineries or shipping facilities. It could also be an aggressive strategy depending on the leaders' motivation.

A third kind of acquisition is undertaken to create diversity. Unlike the internal growth strategy which develops new products within its own operations, acquisition involves the purchase of a separate company.

Again, this can be a defensive manoeuvre in response to economic conditions. Company leaders may intend to stabilize their organization with the addition of complementary businesses.

Managers of change in companies which grow by acquisition, regardless of kind, deal with highly complex issues. Before, during and after purchase, there is a continual flux in personnel, products, finance, markets, and facilities. It is very important for managers of change to identify essential long-term company values which underlie the newly enlarged company. Politics of change are most delicate in companies which grow through acquisition. Although a seemingly aggressive strategy for growth, aggressive behaviour among managers of change will not necessarily be rewarded. Other company cultural issues should be taken into account.

Managers in the highly diversified environment of the acquisitive company should emphasize communication and creation of a paper trail rationalizing every aspect of a project for change. Loyalty to one product or one company in the group of companies is less important than demonstration of individual and team competence in achieving necessary goals. The skilled manager of people moves most easily from one organizational sub-culture to another. Particularly when managing a major change, a change team should avoid being identified with a single special interest. This undermines their overall effectiveness within the company group.

Disinvestment
This strategy is a defensive tactic when a company must divest itself of assets in order to survive. In this case, it is not a *growth strategy*. In fact, it indicates maintenance of the company's status quo, at best, and negative growth, at worst. Those responsible for change in this instance should encourage colleagues to reframe their situation in positive terms. They should emphasize a team approach through every aspect of the project. Morale is vital when managing this kind of change.

Another form of disinvestment strategy is cyclical, rather than an isolated response to a problem situation. Cyclical disinvestment is a high-risk strategy. It refers to the purchase of companies in order to break them up for their asset value. When managing change in this kind of environment, managers should be prepared for sudden alterations to their projects or dissolution of their initiatives without notice. Initiators of disinvestment strategy are the most aggressive among managers. In the 'eighties they were called 'corporate raiders', and for good reason.

The disinvestment environment is best suited to the emotionally stable and personally calm manager. Interpersonal issues of resentment, low morale, anger and frustration are commonly experienced in companies with this kind of growth strategy. Managers with an entrepreneurial attitude thrive when managing change in these companies.

Understanding strategy

Recognizing a company's historic pattern of growth offers managers valuable information about the context in which change occurs. Assuming that they want their initiative to succeed, they need to discover how best to integrate change and also how to adapt their leadership behaviour to cooperate with this company context.

Aggressive managers in a company with low-risk growth strategies are less likely to influence change than those managers who adopt a more cautious leadership style. Alternatively, those companies which grow using highly combative methods do not reward diplomatic and caring managers. Such leaders will experience considerable stress when managing change in aggressive companies. Any manager whose personal style is seriously at odds with the company culture should question how effective they can be as managers of change within that environment.

Do goals match company needs?

The purpose of this chapter has been to emphasize the importance of company resources, market edge, history and growth strategy when managing change. Any initiative should be integrated into the larger company context if it is to succeed. Still at issue is how to evaluate whether a goal for change matches the company's overall need.

This section concentrates on this. The following activity has three parts. Part 1 evaluates company context. Part 2 refers to the goal for change developed in Activity 5 (page 23). Part 3 compares the answers about context with those about the goal for change. From this can be gained a sense of whether the goal matches the overall needs of the company.

Activity 9

Part 1

Please answer these questions as objectively as possible.

1 Think of five single words which characterize your company.
2 What, if any, qualities of leadership succeed consistently in your company?
3 What, if any, qualities of leadership are not rewarded consistently in your company?
4 What values and principles underlie the company?
5 Does this company exhibit high or low risk in its growth strategy?

```
     1  ----------------------------------------------------------- 5
     low                                                         high
```

6 What is the company vision?

Part 2

Please answer these questions in terms of the goal for change you developed in Activity 5 (page 23).

1 Think of five single words which characterize this goal for change.
2 To manage this change successfully, what leadership skills do you need?
3 Does this change create high or low internal risk for the company's:

- products   1 ------------------------------------- 5
             low   high
- facilities   1 ------------------------------------- 5
             low   high
- people   1 ------------------------------------- 5
             low   high
- finance   1 ------------------------------------- 5
             low   high
- markets   1 ------------------------------------- 5
             low   high

4 Does this change create high or low external risk for the company in terms of:

- government   1 ------------------------------------- 5
             low   high
- social values   1 ------------------------------------- 5
             low   high
- consumer need   1 ------------------------------------- 5
             low   high
- competition   1 ------------------------------------- 5
             low   high
- technology   1 ------------------------------------- 5
             low   high

5 How does this change contribute to company vision?

Part 3

1 Look carefully at the answers in Parts 1 and 2. Are there any contradictions, that is, does the goal for change match vision and overall company strategy?
2 If you can identify any aspects of the goal which are at odds with the company context, focus on these. Reframe these aspects as if they enhanced the company context.
3 If there are serious potential problems with this goal, take time to refine it further. Draw on change team members to improve the goal for change.

Summary

This chapter emphasizes the importance of taking a wide view of company needs before committing to a single goal for change. This examination potentially reveals areas where the goal for change falls short of serving the company as a whole. The case study illustrates that change can indirectly affect the company's strength by overlooking challenges to the company's values and founding principles. There are four questions which can guide an analysis of company context. These lead to an assessment of company resources and strengths. Market edge is defined, and the questions in Activity 7 help to develop a statement of market edge for individual companies.

The skills of framing and reframing are also presented. These emphasize the need for flexible thinking among managers of change. An open-minded assessment of company growth strategy is advised. Tactics appropriate to each strategy are suggested toward refining the goal for change developed in the previous chapter's Activity 5. Finally, Activity 9 highlights the need to match the goal for change to overall company needs.

Selected reading

Edelman, Murray, *The Symbolic Uses of Politics*. Chicago: University of Chicago Press, 1967.

Gainer, Leila J., 'Making the Competitive Connection', *Training and Development Journal*. September 1989.

Merry, Uri and Brown, George I., *Neurotic Behavior of Organizations*. Cleveland, OH: Gardner, 1986.

Miles, R.E. and Snow, C.C., *Organizational Strategy, Structure, and Process*. New York: McGraw-Hill, 1978.

Naisbitt, John, *Megatrends*. New York: Warner, 1982.

4 Plan and implement change

Introduction

Within many large firms it is common practice to separate the activities of planning change from those of implementing it. Plans are developed by one group and implementation is carried out by another. Those who make plans traditionally have higher status than those who put them into practice. There is a logic to this because the two activities depend upon different skills, and many managers specialize in just one of these. Unfortunately—and perhaps illogically—change efforts organized in this way are prone to communication breakdown, end-goal misunderstanding and failed aspects of implementation.

Change initiatives succeed when they are based on the current realities of company life. Proposals and suggestions which overlook staffing shortages, equipment needs or time limitations are impractical and unrealistic. Effective plans for change are developed when such implementation realities are taken into account. This allows recognition that there is a difference between the ideals of what could happen and the facts of what does.

Planners who are unfamiliar or out of touch with the practical details of a situation can hardly be expected to guess it right when developing plans. If those who are planning change are to be effective, they need to 'get their hands dirty'. In any firm, this means that senior managers understand application requirements and involve those who implement changes in the planning process. The more important the change, the more crucial it is to gain input from every available source about the possible impacts of the change. The task is always to narrow the gap between planning ideas and implementation realities.

This applies to corporate-level strategy as well as to shop-floor decisions. Strategic choices made at the director level need the same degree of common sense and use of systems as do those made for operation management. The only real difference is the extent of the damage when plans go wrong.

Part 1
Planning:
preparing for
change

Planned change

> **A plan for change** is an outline of specific actions, set within a time-frame. It includes the names of individuals responsible for these actions, describes how activities will be monitored, and sets criteria for the completed project.

Those who argue in favour of spontaneity should remember that written plans give colleagues the information they need to create change. Documentation also allows consistent monitoring of the project and the means to evaluate the benefits of any actions taken. While over-planning to the point of procrastination is to be avoided, this is actually a rare occurrence in business. More commonly, managers launch into time- and cost-expensive initiatives without actually thinking them through to find the best solutions. Like gambling with company money, managing change in this way is a dangerous idea. The need to act must be balanced with the need to plan.

Case study

Ford Motor Company Limited

> **The purpose of this case study is to illustrate the importance of planning change. The manager involved emphasizes thinking through new ideas in order to discover areas of weakness and strength.**

Team building is an important initiative for Ford Motor Company. Tony Lewis, former Manager of Education and Training for Ford in Europe, has long suggested that team work will help ensure Ford's future success. This requires a change from an individualistic to a team-oriented approach, with new styles of leadership and communication. Tony addresses this kind of challenge by planning for it.

He says, 'When introducing any new intervention, you owe it to yourself and the company to run through as many different scenarios as possible. Planning change requires running various possibilities through your head and looking at their extremes, asking yourself: what are the implications if the change is a success or a failure? Is it the greatest thing that ever happened to the company or the worst? As for the worst possible scenario, it is very difficult to get people to imagine a bad outcome for their ideas. They seem unable to see potential for an unmitigated disaster.'

In 1990, Tony met with the Ford plant management team in South Wales. These managers recognized a need to do things differently just as Tony was preparing to launch a team-building programme. The outcome of this discussion was a series of courses, 'Team Building for Team Leaders', to be offered to those responsible for the manufacture of the Zeta engine. They set goals of: promoting leadership which builds trust and a team orientation; using a common language and method for team building throughout the plants; and creating a positive impact on Zeta engine production through improved communication and work relationships.

The training goals for team building dovetailed with the business goals of plant management. About this, Tony says, 'The more you know about the visions of change existing in the organization, the more able you are to tap into the positive ground swell or avoid the negative stumbling blocks. You have to ask what change would you really like to see? At the same time, you can never put too much investment into upstream planning. This must be toward gathering information and determining new options.'

Tony challenges the idea that a single individual can make change happen in an organization. 'There are times when individual managers are given a mandate from a higher level. They essentially have two choices: to obey the letter of the mandate or to explore all the possible alternative actions which meet the mandate's requirements while also serving the organization long term. The second choice is a process orientation to planning and benefits from collaboration and team work. This is the most beneficial response a manager can offer.'

Developing a team approach in the highly competitive automotive industry is an ongoing challenge. The team building programme, and other steps taken in South Wales plants, show that adequate planning and the ability to adapt to changing circumstances contribute to successful change.

Strengths— weaknesses— opportunities— threats

Feasible and realistic plans are based on an understanding of the company's current conditions. Just as Tony Lewis and his team examine an idea for change so that they discover its strengths and weaknesses, so should any manager who is responsible for major change. Goals should also be assessed to discover any potential opportunities and threats. The process of examining an idea's strengths, weaknesses, opportunities and threats is a common practice in business planning, and this analysis is usually referred to by its acronym SWOT.

Unfortunately, managers generally think of SWOT analysis as a meaningless exercise. Although it is a recognized part of basic management training, it is often presented as a concept rather than a practical technique. In fact, SWOT analysis is a flexible and useful tool for planning change. It can be applied while driving the car, waiting for a train, or out walking the dog. For individuals, it only requires think-time and a pencil and paper. For teams, it needs a willingness among group members to debate the issues and record their results.

Essentially, when applying SWOT to change management, every positive feature of a proposed change is examined as if it were a negative. This is done with the intention of improving plans. One beneficial question would be: 'If someone I basically mistrust proposed this change, what would I say about it?' Answers can reveal weaknesses to ideas for change. By discovering difficulties, back-up measures can be developed to resolve them. Alternatively, every negative feature about the change can be assessed to discover how to transform it into a positive aspect. The framing techniques in the previous chapter's Activity 8 (page 41) contribute to this purpose. New insights then add value to plans for change.

Strengths and weaknesses

According to research findings, managers typically use three methods to examine strengths and weaknesses within their companies. These three are: actual past experience, company 'wisdom' and personal opinion, and competitors' opinion. In 1976, Howard Stevenson of Harvard University asked a number of managers how often they used each of these methods when deciding the strengths and weaknesses of an idea. This chart summarizes the results.

Table 4.1   *Methods of examining strengths and weaknesses*

Managers	Strengths	Weaknesses
Used actual past experience to identify	10% of the time	90% of the time
Used company 'wisdom' to identify	79% of the time	21% of the time
Used competitors' opinion to identify	67% of the time	33% of the time

These results show that managers examine past events 90 per cent of the time when studying weaknesses, and only 10 per cent of the time when analysing company strengths. Alternatively, they rely on their own personal opinion and generally accepted company 'wisdom' 79 per

cent of the time when identifying strengths and 21 per cent when identifying weaknesses. Finally, managers refer to competitors' opinion 67
per cent of the time when determining their own company's strengths
and 33 per cent when considering company weaknesses. This leads to
the conclusion that personal opinion and guesswork are the manager's
methods of choice when identifying strengths, while hard data and
analysis of past events are relied upon to discover and analyse the
company's weaknesses.

This appears to be common sense because strengths do not pose a
threat to the company, while weaknesses do. Also, it takes time to
assess past events, and this time can be spent in discovering and reme-
dying weaknesses, not gloating over strengths. The thinking behind this
suggests that a manager can estimate company strengths from personal
experience and the general comments of customers, and so this
approach saves valuable time. Unfortunately, this view is not always
correct. Human perceptions are subject to human error.

An incomplete assessment of strengths can lead managers to develop
tunnel vision. What is an obvious strength in 1990 can become a serious
weakness in the year 2000. It is as important to study past events and
examine data concerning a company's strengths as it is to analyse its
weaknesses. Chapter 2 presents five business areas (page 19) which can
guide the analysis of internal company matters. These are products and
services, people, facilities, markets, and finance.

Opportunities and threats

A company's external environment offers ongoing opportunities for
growth as well as threats to stability. Any change arising from government, social values, consumer need, technology or competitors can have
a positive or negative impact on the company. For lack of a crystal ball,
managers must thoroughly analyse these five external forces (please
refer to Chapter 2, page 22 for details) when planning change.

The outside environment powerfully influences events inside the company
and should be included in the planning process as much as possible.
Unfortunately, this is extremely difficult. Elections bring unforeseen
changes in government policy, scientific discoveries revolutionize products,
and new rivals invade company markets. All of this can occur without
warning. Even so, leaders who are actively involved in their community
and their industry stay abreast of social change. Although they cannot
prepare for everything, they can maintain the mental flexibility they
need to adjust to sudden and radical social shifts. Because internal business matters seem more readily controlled, they more often draw the
attention of managers. Leaders need to remind themselves to give equal
time to external forces and thoroughly study potential opportunities and
threats from outside sources.

Adapting SWOT to change

Most goals for change include several priority issues. These refer to both the internal and external conditions of the company. Each priority issue should go through a SWOT analysis. Among the questions to be addressed are:

- What actions does this issue require?
- What details must be included?
- How should this be communicated? To whom?
- Who is responsible? To do what? By when?
- How is action to be monitored?

The answers to these questions lead to a list of actions which form the basis of a plan for change.

Generally, those features of the goal which refer to internal matters are assessed as strengths or weaknesses. Those resulting from external forces are considered to pose opportunities or threats. After framing an internal feature as a strength (please refer to Chapter 3, page 40), it should then be reframed as a weakness as well. This avoids complacency or tunnel vision about the 'good news' of change. In the same way, identified weaknesses should be reframed as strengths. This provides insight for developing positive action steps to improve these weaknesses. External features of the goal which present potential opportunities should also be reframed as threats. This leads to the discovery of any danger zones for the change in order to prepare for them. Also, those features which seem to pose threats to the company should be reframed as opportunities. This process, at the least, is a confidence-builder and encourages a pro-active response to threatening situations.

Each recognized strength, weakness, opportunity and threat can contribute practical actions to a plan for change. The following pages offer a guide for SWOT analysis. Questions are provided to analyse goals and organize information about the change. The section following this SWOT analysis, 'Planning: Action Steps', explains how to use information from SWOT to produce a detailed plan for change.

The example to illustrate use of SWOT is taken from the goal-setting section of Chapter 2 (page 18). This goal for change referred to a company's need to meet new safety regulations. The goal statement read:

'We aim to change present safety standards so that they meet new regulations. Previous budget decisions must be evaluated in terms of added costs and possible operational down-time. Understandings must be reached between management and labour about mutual benefits.'

One feature of this goal suggests that the change could be beneficial to both management and labour. This idea of 'mutual benefit' is analysed as a *strength* and a *weakness* in the following SWOT analysis. The feature of 'meeting new regulations' is used to illustrate the *opportunity* and *threat* sections of the SWOT.

Strengths

Goal for change

'We aim to change present safety standards so that they meet new regulations. Previous budget decisions must be evaluated in terms of added costs and possible operational down-time. Understandings must be reached between management and labour about mutual benefits.'

What is one strength of this goal?

Management and labour must reach an understanding.

What needs to be defined about this strength?

What are the specific benefits to management and labour?

Who should define this? How? By when?

Change management team. From safety code information and interviews of affected operators and managers. Immediately.

Who should be told about this strength?

1 Plant staff in general.
2 Those directly affected.

3 Company headquarters.
4 Other divisions in the group.

How should they be told?

1 Notice board, meetings.
2 Personal letters listing benefits of the change.

3 Memo with preliminary plans.
4 Newsletter, press release, notice boards.

By when?

1 When plan is complete.
2 When plan is complete.

3 When plan is complete.
4 After response from headquarters.

Who is responsible for communicating to these groups? When?

The change team. When plan is complete.

Who monitors this process? What data are needed?

A delegate from change team. Effects of the change on staff.

How to collect it?

Confidential interviews and surveys.

Weaknesses

Goal for change

'We aim to change present safety standards so that they meet new regulations. Previous budget decisions must be evaluated in terms of added costs and possible operational down-time. Understandings must be reached between management and labour about mutual benefits.'

What is one weakness of this goal?

Management and labour must reach an understanding.

What needs to be defined about this weakness?

Can these benefits be interpreted as manipulation of facts?

Who should define this? How? By when?

The change team. By approaching consistently negative managers and operators for input as well as positive and pro-active people. Immediately.

Who should be told about this weakness?

1 Ombudsmen and all those administering the change.
2 Those affected by the change.

How should they be told?	**By when?**
1 Personal communication	Immediately.
2 In letter describing benefits.	Immediately.

Who is responsible for communicating to these groups? When?

The change team when plan is complete.

Who monitors this process?	**What data are needed?**
A delegate from change team.	Effects of the change on staff.

How to collect them?

Confidential interviews and surveys.

Opportunities

Goal for change

'We aim to change present safety standards so that they meet new regulations. Previous budget decisions must be evaluated in terms of added costs and possible operational down-time. Understandings must be reached between management and labour about mutual benefits.'

What is one opportunity resulting from this goal?

Adherence to government regulations.

What needs to be defined about this opportunity?

1 Press release announcing the company's commitment to safety.
2 Any potential for tax rebate or special consideration.
3 Aid for recruitment of skilled labour.

Who should define this? How? By when?

The change team. By brainstorming for suggestions. Immediately.

Who should be told about this opportunity?

The marketing department, senior executives, personnel.

How should they be told? By when?

Memos, listing suggestions and dates by which the change team will follow up. Immediately.

Who is responsible for communicating to these groups? When?

The change team. Immediately.

Who monitors this process?

A delegate from change team.

What data are needed?

Effects of the change on public.

How to collect them?

Follow-up interviews of officials, sample of public opinion.

Threats

Goal for change

'We aim to change present safety standards so that they meet new regulations. Previous budget decisions must be evaluated in terms of added costs and possible operational down-time. Understandings must be reached between management and labour about mutual benefits.'

What is one threat resulting from this goal?

Adherence to government regulations.

What needs to be defined about this threat?

1 Likelihood of future regulations contradicting these.
2 Whether production or other areas can or should be reorganized to avoid the need for these regulations.

Who should define this? How? By when?

The change team. By brainstorming for suggestions, meeting with government officials, and interviewing production staff. Immediately.

Who should be told about this threat?

Senior executives, production staff.

How should they be told? By when?

Personal communication and presentations to decision-making meetings. Immediately.

Who is responsible for communicating to these groups? When?

The change team. Immediately.

Who monitors this process?	**What data are needed?**
A delegate from change team.	Effects of the change on public.

How to collect them?

Follow-up interviews of officials, sample of public opinion.

Planning: action steps

A team session Ideally, a team works together when analysing a goal for change. By including more points of view, the opportunity of creating a successful plan becomes increasingly likely. A team approach works best when a facilitator encourages the group to analyse their goal so that they separate each of its features. The team's suggestions are written on flipchart paper and hung on the wall for the whole team to see. Each feature of the goal should be written out in this way. The session also includes framing and reframing each internally related feature of the goal as *both a strength and a weakness*, and each externally related feature as *both an opportunity and a threat*.

A list of these strengths, weaknesses, opportunities and threats is then given to each individual member of the team. Team members take this away and individually answer the SWOT analysis questions. How to apply these questions is illustrated on the preceding pages. These questions are also repeated as fill-in-the-blank forms in Activity 10 which follows. Separate SWOT sheets should be completed for each strength, weakness, opportunity and threat which the group members identify. Later, the team brings their sheets to a follow-up planning meeting for further discussion within the whole group.

This approach yields a maximum contribution of new ideas for the development of action steps. Together the group answers the SWOT questions. Because they have already done this as individuals, discussion and debate occur more readily. From this, the team builds up a comprehensive list of what needs to be done. The action steps they generate are then collated into a manageable format: what to do, who does it, by when. These steps collectively form their action plan. Whenever possible, SWOT should be carried out by teams. This approach minimizes the effects of bias and tunnel vision when planning change.

Activity 10 *Please return to the goal for change which you developed in Activity 3 (page 19).*

1 Use the following SWOT questions to analyse each feature of your goal for change.
2 Make a list of all the actions you include in your answers, emphasizing who is responsible and by when.
3 Make a list of all monitoring actions: data, methods of collection, and who is responsible.

Strengths *Goal for change*

What is one strength of this goal?

What needs to be defined about this strength?

Who should define this? How? By When?

Who should be told about this strength?

How should they be told?

By when?

Who is responsible for communicating to these groups? When?

Who monitors this process? What data are needed? How to collect them?

Weaknesses   *Goal for change*

What is one weakness of this goal?

What needs to be defined about this weakness?

Who should define this? How? By when?

Who should be told about this weakness?

How should they be told? By when?

Who is responsible for communicating to these groups? When?

Who monitors this process? What data are needed?

How to collect them?

Opportunities   *Goal for change*

What is one opportunity resulting from this goal?

What needs to be defined about this opportunity?

Who should define this? How? By when?

Who should be told about this opportunity?

How should they be told? By when?

Who is responsible for communicating to these groups? When?

Who monitors this process? What data are needed?

How to collect them?

Threats   *Goal for change*

What is one threat resulting from of this goal?

What needs to be defined about this threat?

Who should define this? How? By when?

Who should be told about this threat?

How should they be told? By when?

Who is responsible for communicating to these groups? When?

Who monitors this process? What data are needed?

How to collect them?

Problem—
analysis—
discussion

Problem

A security blind manufacturing company, based in northern England, recently acquired a French firm which supplies its locks and fittings. The UK company president negotiated the deal on impulse after learning that the French firm was suffering a severe cash crisis. His intention was to ensure a constant supply of specialized equipment.

The security blind company is run on paternalistic lines. The president is also father and uncle to the entire management team. While major issues are debated and decisions put to a vote, the final choice is always made by the president. The lock company purchase was made without the knowledge of either the Finance Director or the Vice President of Operations, who are also the president's sons.

The Operations Vice President is seriously concerned because the demand for their blinds has decreased during the previous year and they are carrying much more stock than expected. At a time when they should act to conserve their own cash, his father has purchased a source of lock supply for which they have a limited need, at least for the present.

The Finance Director is equally worried. During the last six months he has repeatedly warned his father about the company's own cash problems. His proposals for reducing overheads and cutting expenses have fallen on deaf ears. By purchasing a company with severe cash problems, he has added an unwelcome burden to their own situation.

Analysis

In this case a major change occurred without planning. Imagine yourself in the position of company president just as he learned that their French supplier was in trouble. Please answer the following questions having recognized that your preferred choice is to buy the French firm immediately.

1 Can I identify blind spots which influence my choice?
2 What choices would my fellow managers (and family) make?
3 List the strengths of my choice and of any alternatives.
4 List the weaknesses of my choice and of any alternatives.
5 List the opportunities from my choice and alternatives.
6 List the threats from my choice and alternatives.

ussion The company president in this case is in the habit of taking immediate action. As its founder, he created the firm's original success. It should also be added, though, that its product was in heavy demand during the company's formative years. Any mistakes he made as a manager were balanced by the high turnover and profits from consistent sales.

Now that the company's sales have decreased, its management team must develop a strategy that minimizes mistakes and draws on the collected wisdom of the whole management team. They can't afford a hit or miss approach. SWOT analysis would be a useful technique to test ideas before actually implementing them even though this approach would challenge impulse and limit spontaneity. During times of crisis or decreasing resources, SWOT provides a means of reducing risk and adding security to decisions about change.

The company president should have examined more fully his impulse to buy the lock producer. He certainly should have conferred with his management team. A SWOT analysis could have led to the development of a more local source of supply, with resulting cost saving. Another alternative to buying the firm would have been the purchase of licensing rights for a local manufacturer to make the locks or buying a share of the French firm's patent. Studying the strengths, weaknesses, opportunities and threats of an idea for change inevitably generates alternative choices.

Part 2
Implementation:
making change
happen

Implementation
issues

> **Implementing change** means acting on ideas. Individuals perform tasks toward achieving the plans they made for change. Ideally, this occurs within a time-frame and is monitored against agreed performance standards.

The best conceived plans for change have value only if they are acted upon. They are likely to be successful if the ongoing effects of change are monitored and plans are adjusted as necessary. Particularly when managing the people aspects of change, it is a good idea to consider in advance the impact of every action taken.

Case study

The Prudential Assurance Company Limited

> The purpose of this case study is to illustrate the importance of total employee involvement in the change process. The manager involved describes completing the approval process for British Standard 5750 in record time.

The display of the 'Registered Firm' symbol for British Standard 5750 assures clients that a company maintains a rigorous quality assurance system. The application for this quality standard can take as long as 24 months, because some companies must reorganize before necessary quality control procedures are in place. Prudential Assurance Industrial Branch Life Administration division completed this approval process in just six months. This result is an impressive achievement and a first for the insurance industry.

Dr Stephen Tanner, Quality Initiative Manager, coordinated this project. He knew that previously undertaken quality initiatives within Life Administration ensured their customers received high quality service and strove for continuous improvement. BS 5750 announces that fact to the general public and increases competitiveness.

He says, 'When we decided to go for BS 5750, we knew there were other insurance companies after it as well. Our plan was to get our people totally involved in the process and also to be first. It wouldn't be a case of a project team doing it for them, we wanted the staff to write the procedures for themselves. This way we would know that the written procedures accurately describe what is actually done. This needed a major motivational effort so that people wanted registration and were 100 per cent behind the process. It took six months to prepare for the British Standards audit, and two months of that was planning.'

Industrial Branch Life Administration has 250 staff organized into levels of senior managers, divisional heads, supervisors and clerical staff. The plan involved forming teams of mixed organizational levels and asking experienced clerical staff—just below supervisor level—to manage the teams. Their selection served three purposes. First, it gave them experience that they wouldn't normally have; second, it was time-saving for management level; and third, it provided insight into the pressure which managers regularly experience.

After nomination, the team leaders were invited to a briefing meeting where BS 5750 was explained. Steve told them that the goal was to achieve it in just six months. Their initial reaction was sceptical, but when they learned that no one had ever done it before, they became inspired by the idea of going for it.

'A key driver to get the staff involved was pride. The Industrial Branch Life Administration area is sometimes considered to be out of the mainstream by some within the company, dealing with an old-fashioned kind of insurance. In fact, they are really good at what they do. We told them this and said that achieving registration would show how good they are. This way they tapped into their own need for recognition which, after all, is something we all want.'

Preparation for the audit involved using competitions, giving prizes, displaying checklists and other visual aids. The team leaders' task was to rally all the staff in teams and draft procedures that describe their work processes. The next stage required those staff to assess the accuracy of their written procedures. After making necessary revisions, they underwent an internal audit conducted by independent consultants. From this, they learned which areas needed further improvement.

Steve believes that they achieved registration in rapid time because they had total people involvement in the whole of the process. 'By the time we underwent the actual British Standards Institution audit, the staff were so motivated to pass that it was impossible for us to fail. This is what we wanted: that the staff would own the process themselves, enjoy the experience of quality work. You can force people to follow standard procedures by threatening them with trouble if the BSI auditors catch them, but then staff won't follow the standards unless you police them. In the end, you lose the benefits of quality assurance, like customer satisfaction and the drive for continuous improvement.'

Envisioning results

Symbol of success   Working with change can be frustrating because by its nature change is ongoing and never complete. As each action in business creates a reaction, even a completed change continues to be developed and modified as the company interacts with its customers and the competition. For example, even state-of-the-art equipment needs regular upgrading, its operators need training and managers of change need to modify and adjust their plans accordingly.

Unfortunately, announcing to colleagues that change never stops often decreases their motivation rather than stimulates them to greater effort. Steve Tanner and his colleagues encouraged their division to go after BS 5750 by providing clear end-goals for each stage of the process. Even though the whole team would acknowledge that the pursuit of quality never ends, the staff kept themselves motivated by achieving tangible 'end-stages' at intervals during the process.

Alternatively, imagine a situation where two managers, one senior and one junior, are sitting together after a meeting during which staff cuts were announced. The senior manager, in a philosophical mood, sits back and says reflectively, 'Change is an ongoing process. It never ends.' Many employees would join the junior manager in wondering, 'What is the boss saying? Am I the next to go?'

It is a healthy practice for change teams to imagine the real-life events which result from their plans. By doing so, they create a vision for the future that is grounded in the realities of the company. Managers who cannot describe a proposed change in this way can hardly expect their colleagues to understand fully what is expected of them. Imagining the details of a change and also its potential outcome is difficult but is ultimately beneficial.

A plan which gives clear criteria to mark the 'end' of a change is easier to manage. Office computerization provides a good example because this innovation is readily adapted into several planning stages. First, there is the choice of equipment and training schemes. Second, the equipment arrives and a core group of staff is trained. Third, the current client files are computerized, along with a decided number of past files. This third stage can be considered an 'ending point' for the project and can provide the staff with a reason to congratulate themselves.

Even though training is still ongoing and all records are not as yet entered into the database, this artificial ending point gives those involved in the change a psychological breathing space. It is important to recognize this human need for completion. To ignore it undervalues employees' efforts in a subtle way, and risks suggesting that they are taken for granted.

Instead, they should be told regularly and often that their effort makes a valuable contribution to the company. Genuine thanks, respect and recognition of a difficult job, well done, is often more appreciated by staff than cash incentives. All of this argues in favour of choosing an event which would mark the closure of a project. This event functions as a sign and symbol of success.

Often, a symbol of success is interpreted as a suggestion to have a party. Although celebrations are often appropriate, the symbol should relate to the project itself. It is a specific event which signals that a stage of the change has come to an end. The use of symbols is more fully explained in the next section.

What is a symbol?

A symbol provides a visual image and is a powerful means for presenting a goal for change. In the office computerization example, a symbol for successful completion could be the final removal of banks of dusty filing cabinets and the increased space in the office. This symbol gives staff a common purpose toward which they can direct their efforts and attention. When frustration builds up or disruption is at its worst, the manager says, 'Imagine how much better we will feel when we are free of those dusty filing cabinets.'

Symbols are most effective when they provide positive images. The suggestion of 'removing dusty filing cabinets' creates a mental picture. A less successful symbol for the project's completion would be, 'Imagine how much better we will feel when the new system allows us to improve retrieval capacity by 50 per cent.' It is difficult to visualize 'improvement' or 'file retrieval capacity' or '50 per cent'. This is because they are *ideas*, not *images*.

Images emerge from the right side of our brain, which is spatially and pictorially oriented. The right brain is entirely interpretive and recognizes only positive messages. For example, if you are told not to imagine a black bear or not to think about eating lunch, the right brain 'hears' the message as 'imagine a black bear' and 'think about eating lunch'.

Rational thought, language, and analysis of information emerges from the left side of the brain. When you and your team *discuss the merits* of using a symbol of success, you use left-brain, thinking processes. Many business leaders are dominated by left-brain, analytical thinking. As a result, they may underestimate the powerful influence which symbols have on everyone, including themselves. This bias can inhibit their ability to use symbols effectively when evoking their colleagues' support for a project. It can also limit their ability to describe a project's successful outcome in visual terms.

Change implementation benefits from the use of symbols. A first attempt at choosing an image may produce an ineffective left-brain effort. Go after robust and colourful pictures of success. Draw your colleagues into the process so that you create a symbol which makes everyone say, 'Yes, we want that.' Of course, this is more difficult when change leads to widespread redundancy. In this case, consider using a symbol for out-going employees which encourages their re-employment. Then ask the team to choose a different symbol for motivating the remaining staff, one which reminds them to pull together for mutual benefit.

Whatever the symbol, it serves its purpose best if it is publicized. All of those involved in the change should know what a successful outcome would look like, sound like and feel like. This is a powerful tool for encouraging everyone to work toward a common goal. It is also an opportunity for leaders to show a clear vision for a changed future.

Activity 11

Please return to the goal which you developed in Activity 9 (page 46). Answer these questions toward discovering an appropriate symbol for the goal's success.

1 What outcome of this change would you value most?
2 What outcome would your colleagues value most?
3 What is the best outcome overall? Please be specific.
4 What will company employees say about this change when it is finally in place?
5 What quality would the change demonstrate, for example, cooperation, creativity, discipline, etc.?
6 Is there a specific word, phrase or event which could symbolize this change in the company?
7 How will you and your team promote this symbol?

The audience profile

The audience profile is used to organize information about the people involved in a change effort. This information emerges from the SWOT analysis questions which identify the groups involved in the change. A profile of each of these groups aids communication and defines the need for regular contact. It also leads to decisions about training issues, policy statements and recognition of procedural needs. When these are considered in advance of publicizing a major change, then this 'human dimension' of information can be provided along with the announcement of the change.

In line with their company's general goals, every group or department has different priorities and interests based on their functions and work requirements. Tact and diplomacy should be used when presenting goals for change to these groups, particularly in written messages. To illustrate this, refer again to the goal used as an example for the SWOT analysis in Part 1 of this chapter (page 54). It included several features: one of these related to people issues, 'labour and management' and another to finance, 'added costs'.

When announcing this goal, it is essential that the same message be given to everyone. It is appropriate, though, to highlight the feature which has most relevance to a specific department or group. For example, finance departments are traditionally suspicious of change which emphasizes improvements solely for people. Because they are directly responsible for managing cash-flow, they are cautious about new ideas which are not aimed to generate income. The memo or announcement about change sent to this group could include a 'Special Remarks' section, with the message that 'Your cost analysis input is appreciated as vital to the decision-making process.' The effect of this short message is to assure them that their work is valued and their concerns are included in the planning process.

Alternatively, the main concerns for the production department are different. To emphasize the importance of cost analysis to this group is like waving a red flag at a bull. Instead, a 'Special Remarks' section of their memo or announcement would point out that 'Input from both operators and managers is needed to make the right decisions about implementing the new safety regulations. Your cooperation is very much appreciated.'

Although the same basic memo about the need to meet new regulations goes out to everyone, the special interests of individual groups are acknowledged. If this seems manipulative, that is not the intention. There are managers who believe that they show integrity when they speak to everyone in the same way. They want to show all their staff the same degree of respect. While their intentions are good, they are tactically mistaken. In fact, they ignore the fact that there are varying priorities and different driving interests within every department. The manager's task is to create harmony from these differences, not ignore them.

Adjusting the message to meet the interests of the audience allows a manager to work more effectively with the different needs of each group or individual. Recognizing differences increases the likelihood that colleagues *experience* the respect which a manager intends to give them. It is often not enough to mean well when managing change. Understanding the audience and addressing their concerns and interests improves leadership performance.

Audience profile questions

These questions should be answered for each group identified in the SWOT analysis completed in Activity 10 (page 59).

Identify the group.

How important is this group for implementing the change?

1   <----<----<---->---->----> 　　10
　　low　　　　　　　　　high

Any prominent individuals in the group?
• qualities?
• gender?
• age?

Any prominent characteristics of the group?
• qualities?
• gender?
• age?

Any special interests or priorities to be addressed?
• ambitions?
• fears?
• biases?

Any training or development needs?
• for individuals?
• for the group?

Any blocks to their accepting the change?

Do your feelings toward this group help or hinder your ability to present the change?

Communication: system and strategy

System Managers in powerful positions often do not realize how challenging it is for their staff to implement their plans for change. Even those leaders who have the full confidence and trust of their employees must beware of mistaking this loyalty for complete understanding. Initiating an idea for change differs widely from acting on it. This difference creates a potential gap in communication. When managing change, a well-developed system for giving clear messages to all concerned is essential.

The decision about how messages are circulated within the company is actually as important as what the messages contain. Managers of change should realize that sending or publishing information is not the equivalent of its being received. For example, announcing, 'The minutes are available to everyone on the project', does not address whether the minutes are read.

Colleagues' and employees' work habits should be considered when reviewing how to communicate change. Some useful questions to consider are: Is a meeting attended by only half of a work group the right place to announce major company change? Are memos a reliable means for making information available when it is known that they are rarely read? Do different levels of staff require different communication methods according to their work environments? A thorough analysis of the *context* for communication increases the likelihood of the necessary information actually being received.

Before announcing any message about goals for change, consider these questions and revise the message if necessary. The following questions serve to ensure that a message is clear and meets the needs of its audience.

- What are the essentials of this message?
- What is the most positive interpretation it can receive by the most committed team members?
- What is the most cynical response it can receive?
- What are the biases and special interests of the audience?

Strategy SWOT analysis organizes information about what needs to be communicated. The audience profile highlights the interests of those who receive the information. This section addresses the *methods* by which messages can be given. This leads to choices about a communication strategy for change.

If colleagues mention more than twice that they have not received messages, then managers should review their choice of communication methods. Particularly, when information is vital to the success of a change, back-up methods are important. When delivering messages, it is advisable to use three different methods. For example, the information should appear, first, as a general announcement on a notice board, loudspeaker or in a public meeting. Second, each person affected by the change should receive an individual memo. This highlights any important points, and recipients can refer to their memos later. Third, important changes should also be communicated on a person-to-person basis. This means one-to-one interviews between each person involved in the change and a member of the change team or a designated manager. These meetings provide personalized sources of information and a forum for addressing concerns and answering questions.

The following chart presents eight methods of communication. Each of these is useful and appropriate under specific circumstances. Every manager has a preferred style of contacting their colleagues. In everyday circumstances, following these preferences is an adequate communication strategy. When managing change, this approach leaves too much to chance.

Each of the eight methods is listed in the first of four columns (see Table 4.2). Three other columns refer to the *use* managers make of these

Table 4.2 *Eight methods of communication*

	Presently used	*Effectiveness* 0 = poor 5 = excellent	*Potentially used*
Public address (large group)			
Briefing session (small group)			
Written memo			
One-to-one			
Telephone			
Newsletter			
Bulletin board			
Grapevine			

methods. The first of these three columns addresses 'Presently used' strategies of communication. If any of the eight methods are currently used as part of a communication strategy, then this column should be ticked. The next column, 'Effectiveness: 0 to 5', asks for a score to be given for the overall effectiveness of that method in terms of *everyone* receiving *all* the necessary information *whenever* it is required. The final column, 'Potentially used', refers to methods which could be tried. While the method is not a part of the current communication strategy, it could perhaps enhance the circulation of vital information in the future. If so, then this column should also be ticked.

Communication networks

There are four different kinds of networks which typically exist in organizations. In addition to choosing an appropriate communication method, these four networks, both formal and informal, can serve the development of a communication strategy.

Hierarchy

This network refers to the official roles and titles held by members within the company. Using this network means following company procedure to communicate information. This is the most formal method, and its success depends entirely on the overall quality of communication within the company. If this regularly breaks down, then another network should always be used as a back-up.

Expert

This network refers to the interest and skill groups clustered around the company's specialisms. Using this network means sending information to all geophysicists, all clerical staff, all technical engineers or all consulting surgeons, regardless of their official positions. This is a less formal network. Care must be taken if there is a risk of 'offending' company protocol or members within the hierarchical network.

Influential

This network refers to those who have prestige and power within the company, whether through politics, seniority, skills and talents, family and personal relationships, or charisma. Using this network means making ongoing informal contact toward increasing personal prestige through gaining and giving information. The more this network is used, the more influence is gained within it. It is an informal network and an extremely useful one. Managers of change should actively use this network whenever possible.

Friendship

This network refers to personal friends, family and supporters within the company. Using this network means providing and seeking information as needed to help each other. It is the most informal of the networks. Unlike the influential network, using this one can gradually erode the strength of other contacts within the company. There is a risk of becoming overly identified with one clique or special interest group.

The 'grapevine' within companies is made up of contacts described here as 'Influence' and 'Friendship' networks. These can be very useful when a back-up communication tactic is required.

Activity 12   *Please refer to Activity 11 (page 66) in which you developed a symbol for success. You can use this symbol as an example of a message to be communicated.*

1 What method would you use to announce this message?
2 What communication network would you use?
3 What are the essentials of this message?
4 How is it likely to be received?
5 Can you frame it so that it addresses the audience's interests?

Problem— analysis— discussion

Problem   The owner-director of a cardboard packaging company decided to refurbish the administrative staff's work area. This was a large open-plan office where the company's accounting, sales, purchasing and distribution business was conducted. Staff shared equipment, facilities and clerical support as needed.

Although this atmosphere was pleasantly cooperative, the director believed that his staff deserved a better physical environment and his company an improved image. In the 20 years since the company was founded, the floor covering had become worn, the ceiling stained, lighting outdated, and staff conveniences in poor repair.

To ensure that it would be a surprise for the staff, the director carefully planned all the necessary changes himself. The plan included using the company's slow season in January and February for the changes and moving all the staff into portacabins in the car park. Computer equipment would be based in one cabin, central files in another, and staff would be separated according to their functions.

When he announced the change in December, the staff's reaction astounded him. Far from appreciating the refurbishment as an extra Christmas surprise, they were furious at the idea of the sudden change. Among their complaints was the organization of the portacabins. They argued that well-designed equipment placement was essential to maintain their present level of use. Not only did the plan disrupt their organization, the director seemed not to value the effort they put into the former office arrangement and their spirit of cooperation.

Others were annoyed at the inconvenience of working in cramped facilities during the coldest and wettest part of the year. While they admitted their building was shabby, they didn't want the discomfort that accompanied the change. A disabled employee felt very frustrated at the five-minute wheelchair journey required to use the ladies' facilities located on the far side of the building from the cabins. After hearing from his staff, the director felt very angry and rather hurt.

Analysis *Please imagine yourself in the role of an outside consultant invited to give the director advice after his announcement of the change. Use the following questions to organize information toward helping him to understand what happened and why.*

1 What implementation areas did the director omit?
2 What information would an audience profile have provided?
3 What methods of communication were appropriate for this change?
4 Is there a symbol for success that would have helped promote this change?

Discussion The director didn't realize that the emotional upset of a major change is magnified when it is also announced as a surprise. Because he believed that he knew and understood his staff thoroughly, he omitted studying them as a recipient audience for change. This would have reminded him of the disabled employee and the large number of women staff who also would have to journey to the facilities. His plan could easily have included the hiring of a special unit for these staff and ramps for disabled access.

He could also have managed communication more effectively. Once he realized that the idea of a surprise would not work, he could have invited long-serving staff members to form a change team. They would have enjoyed this participation far more than the element of surprise. Communication methods would have included one-to-one meetings to get individual ideas, a memo to each person with logistical information and a series of short briefing meetings to gather suggestions and inspire support for this project.

Refurbishment lends itself to the use of many different symbols. One of these could have focused on the improved atmosphere from the change, another on colour and light, and a third on the upgraded image for the whole company. An outside consultant faced with this situation should also suggest that the director start again and form a team to implement the change.

Summary This chapter presents stage three of the method for managing change. It suggests that planning ideas and implementation realities should be considered simultaneously. Therefore, both activities are presented as two parts of the same stage. The first part, 'Planning: preparing for change', emphasizes techniques for assessing goals for change. SWOT analysis (strengths, weaknesses, opportunities, and threats) is adapted for change management. A series of questions is provided which guides the creation of an action plan based on SWOT.

The second part, 'Implementation: making change happen', offers techniques to ensure that plans for change are understood and accepted by those who are asked to implement them. These include creation of a symbol for success and conducting a study of training and other needs of those involved in the change. It is suggested that managers of change should avoid assuming that messages about change are understood. Even staff who are committed to the change need constant and clear communication of what is expected of them. Systems and strategies of communication are presented to ensure that plans for change are fully explained to those requiring information.

Selected reading

Argenti, John, *Predicting Corporate Failure*. London: Institute of Chartered Accountants in England and Wales, 1984.

de Bono, Edward, *Lateral Thinking for Management*. New York: Penguin, 1982.

de Bono, Edward, *The Mechanism of Mind*. London: Penguin, 1990.

Gainer, Leila J., 'Making the Competitive Connection', *Training and Development Journal*. September 1989, pp S1–S30.

Mintzberg, Henry and Quinn, James B., *The Strategy Process* (2nd ed.). Englewood Cliffs, NJ: Prentice-Hall, 1991.

Pearce, John A. II and Robinson B. Jr., *Strategic Management: Strategic Formulation and Implementation* (2nd ed.). Homewood, IL: Irwin, 1985.

Sloan Management Review, *Planning Strategies that Work*. Oxford: Oxford University Press, 1987.

Stevenson, Howard H., 'Defining Corporate Strengths and Weaknesses', *Sloan Management Review*. Spring 1976, pp 51–68.

5 Evaluation

Evaluation benefits

The challenge of implementing change often leaves little energy and minimal time for analysis of results. Busy managers complete their final reports and then move rapidly on to their next projects. While they realize the value of in-depth evaluation, they do not always schedule time to do it.

Evaluation adds value to the experience of managing change. It emphasizes learning from all aspects of the effort and leads to decisions about managing future change. An in-depth report documents how the company develops as a result of the change and removes future guesswork about what actually happened. Evaluation contributes to the company's growth because it allows new benefits to be fully appreciated and mistakes to be understood and corrected. A half-hearted or shallow evaluation effort means lost opportunity for learning. When managers say they are too busy to review all aspects of the change process, they undermine their credibility as agents of change and also as fully effective managers.

In the 'Cautionary Tale' of Chapter 1 (page 6), the sector president received a report from the investigating panel. The report's function was to summarize and evaluate data and to propose a plan of action. As the story revealed, the panellists chose to falsify these data and make proposals which served individual rather than company interests. Because the president accepted the report as a fair representation of the panel's findings, he saw no need to seek additional solutions to the company's cash-flow problem.

Managers of change have the task of squeezing the last drop of information from any events which may contribute to the change which they are managing. There were other sources of information available to this president. Among these were: minutes from the panel's discussions, confidential position statements from each member, anonymous surveys, interviews with panellists conducted by neutral outsiders, a personal visit to the last panel meeting, among other suggestions. His job, as convener of the panel, was to assess their evaluation. Time spent on this activity would possibly have saved him weeks of time later as he contributed to the fight against the take-over bid.

Additional information sources are always necessary. Managers of change must recognize that sometimes people are dishonest; at other times they are misguided; but on most occasions they are simply too close to the data to draw the wisest conclusions. A company president as well as a plant manager needs to recognize the importance of evaluating the short- and long-term impact of change at every stage of the change process. Even if a plan has been fully implemented, this doesn't mean it is the best and wisest course of action. It takes courage to question positive results, but in the long run, honest evaluation always adds benefit to the company.

Case study

Scandinavian Airlines

> **The purpose of this case study is to illustrate the importance of on-going evaluation throughout a change project. This manager recognized that a training programme, already underway, needed radical adjustment. She describes the need to study a project's requirements and then evaluate results to discover if these needs are met.**

Scandinavian Airlines launched an initiative in 1991 to change the company from a production to a customer focus orientation. This required training all 20 000 of its employees in a cascade throughout the company. The most senior company leaders emphasized the vital importance of this by personally training 800 other high-level managers in company vision and strategy. This ensured widespread understanding of their goal for change.

Tina Kaplan is responsible for Human Resources and is one of a four-person project group guiding this major initiative. She explains, 'While the training of the 800 managers went on, we also recruited internally 23 potential trainers with a profile of customer focus excellence. To evaluate the many applicants for this trainer position, we designed a two-day seminar so that we could actually live with them. This programme emphasized presentation-giving, problem-solving and interactive games. Rather than interview individuals in a closed room, we chose to watch them interact with people. This gave us the kind of information we needed about their creativity, social and leadership skills.' In this way, the project group chose an evaluation method which matched the needs of their programme.

They wanted to form a group of trainees which had sufficient customer knowledge to help co-design a highly relevant customer focus course. The trainees would use this course to train their 20 000 colleagues and also learn facilitation and presentation skills. To this end, Tina and the project group developed a two-month programme with a detailed curriculum for its first five weeks. With complete confidence, she opened the first session.

'I really believe that we recruited the best people in the company for this programme, but as the first day progressed I realized that something was missing. Our original task from Jan Carlzon, company president and chief executive officer, was to *motivate* people on the front line to focus on the customer. This was a very complex assignment because you cannot *tell* people to be motivated and expect success. These trainees had no idea of the difficulty of this work. Ultimately, we had to train them to empower and inspire their colleagues on the front line, to share even a part of their dedication [to excellent service] and our programme didn't address this.'

This interim evaluation after only one day of training led to a change from programmed to process-oriented learning. With the same end-goal in mind of providing the company with 23 customer focus trainers, Tina adjusted the content of their training to meet the needs of these individuals as those needs would emerge each day. 'I realized that when dealing with this kind of human development, I had to let go of my ideas and let the participants show me what they needed to learn. Rather than impose my original plan for their training, I made a plan of not planning.' She acknowledges that this was a risk, but she also had the necessary skill to guide this challenging process to a successful completion.

Tina expressed caution concerning over-attention to goals while a project is ongoing. 'When you tell someone about a change, they don't always hear it as you mean it. While you must tell them the end-goal and continue to guide the process, you should also leave the next immediate step up to them. The gap between the reality of today and the vision for tomorrow cannot be too great because people become worried that they won't achieve it. We can't stop life and life means change. No matter how turbulent the change is, we have to grab hold and become a part of it, be positive about it. I want to shape the change if I can, not worry about it.'

The 23 seminar leaders continue to train their 20 000 colleagues. Tina describes one sign of the success they have already brought to the project. 'A year ago, if you asked an employee, "Who is paying your salary?" you could hear, "The accounts department", "My boss", "Jan Carlzon". Now the answer is, "the customer". To me this indicates that our change towards customer focus is succeeding.'

What to include in evaluation

Evaluating change is easier if the desired results are identified before the change effort begins. This marks a return to visualizing the outcome of a plan as described in the 'Envisioning results' section of the previous chapter (page 64): a manager should be able to describe how success will look, sound and feel. Clarity about goals allows the evaluation of results. Specific goals lead to clear evaluations. Expressed standards and criteria for achievement allow an honest and realistic review of actual performance.

In the project described by Tina Kaplan, she and her project group needed certain results from their training of the 23 internal trainer candidates. As day one of the programme progressed, Tina identified a gap between the goals established for the training programme and the likely result of the course as she was presenting it on that first day. With courage, she decided to act on this evaluation.

Evaluation methods such as interviews, surveys or statistical measures provide a structure to organize data about the change. For example, when planning an organizational change, those who are involved can be interviewed before and after the change. This provides information about expectations and results. Alternatively, technical changes can also be measured before and after they are in place by using charts, gauges or visual inspection. This provides data about the specific merits of the change. There are three questions which should be addressed when evaluating change. These are:

- What *results* will demonstrate success?
- What *data* can show these results?
- Which *methods* best organize those data?

Answering these questions simplifies the evaluation process. A description of the desired *results* provides an ideal solution against which the actual outcomes of the change can be measured. Knowing what kind of *data* are required to prove success encourages their collection as the change is implemented. In addition, decisions about necessary data guide the choice of *methods* which should be used to collect them.

The development of an action plan, using the guidelines in the previous chapter, includes making a list of all monitoring actions, data requirements, collection methods, and the names of the people responsible for monitoring these actions. This list is the basis for analysing the success of the change. As the project nears completion, all of this information will be available for integration into a report. At the final stage of the change process when there is least time, energy or inclination for creative effort, a prearranged evaluation strategy is available. The result is a comprehensive analysis of the change without loss of momentum after implementation.

Standard company reports

Many companies require managers to follow a standard format for data collection and project evaluation. This guides the kind of information which will be included in a final report about the change. There are obvious benefits to standardized evaluation forms. They save time, provide consistent information, offer ease of entry and access to databases, and ensure a minimum quality for all final reports. This approach also relieves managers of unnecessary stress by providing a general outline and even pre-printed forms for completion.

Difficulties arise when managers want to pass on valuable information, cautions or concerns to colleagues or to senior levels within the company, and the forms do not allow inclusion of any personal response or individual reactions. In such cases, the forms should be supplemented by additional remarks directed at a specific audience. This can take the form of a memo or covering letter with attached summaries of data and descriptions of methods used to obtain them.

In the following pages, suggestions are offered for dealing with difficult issues during evaluation. Managers of change who are limited by standard formats can adapt the ideas to suit their company's needs. Others can use the suggestions to improve their present evaluation process.

Problem— analysis— discussion

Problem A plant manager receives a memo from the divisional head office. He is asked to introduce a new quality inspection procedure to occur at intervals along the production line. Operators are asked to place a mark on a graph when they visually discover faults from an earlier point of assembly. Sheets of graph paper, fixed on clipboards, are located beside each main point of assembly. Traditionally, plant management in this company has not allowed operators to influence the flow of production. When operators have asked for more influence over the production line in the past, company management has forcefully refused. The new visual inspection is the best response offered to the operators so far, although the memo does not authorize them to stop the line or to remove faulty items from it. They are simply to make a mark on the graph.

The plant manager follows the instructions of the memo fully, but he believes this change to be essentially meaningless and potentially damaging to future work relations in the plant. Having implemented the change, he now completes the company's standard evaluation form. This form addresses issues such as the degree to which a change is implemented; the amount of time it took to complete; problems which arose during implementation; and training issues.

The issue of validity or usefulness of the change is not raised in the standard format. The plant manager wants to evaluate both the long-term political impact of quality inspection by operators as well as the reasoning behind charting errors and then doing nothing with the information. He is hindered because he knows that any implied criticism of the idea is potentially damaging to his own promotion prospects. Also, he realizes that he will be blamed if any trouble arises among the plant's employees as a result of the initiative.

Analysis *Imagine yourself in the role of this plant manager. After having fully implemented this change, you decide to express your concerns about the initiative to the head office. You want to be convincing and also diplomatic. The following questions help focus reactions to the initiative.*

1 How can you discover what the head office actually wants to achieve with this quality inspection effort?
2 Having ensured that the operators make their visual inspections, how else can the plant cooperate with a quality initiative?

3 Without stopping the production line, how else can operators identify faults to support the visual method?

4 What data can you collect which show the actual result?
 • from operators?
 • from production figures?
 • from rejected goods?
 • from other plant managers?

5 What methods would you use to collect these data?

Discussion   This manager's situation is a common one in large companies where planning and implementation activities are separate. The memo was written by a head office manager who was promoted from the finance department. His understanding of a quality initiative is identification of faults and reduction of rejects. This manager believes that his idea is an ideal solution: it asks for the charting of errors but avoids rejection of units.

The plant manager's task is to educate this boss and others like him. If he completes an audience profile with the head office management as his sample, he should focus on their concerns and the issues driving them. When he organizes supplementary information about the shortcomings of this quality initiative, his understanding of this audience can improve his communication with them.

Supplementary pages could contain data: about the number of customer complaints both before and after the visual inspection initiative, positive suggestions from operators about the change, new ideas such as tagging faulty parts along with charting their numbers, and other features. The important point is to use objective evaluation measures to convince the head office that quality inspection can be improved. This sidesteps the need to complain about the original visual inspection idea.

How to evaluate change

An in-depth evaluation of change emphasizes four essential points:

 • a summary of the goals and rationale for change
 • a summary of results
 • contrasts between these goals and the results
 • recommendations for the future.

A clear presentation of this information allows informed decision-making for future company development. When using a standard reporting format, an introductory letter and supplementary sections are often needed. The inclusion of this material gives the reader a comprehensive summary of the whole of a change initiative.

Too often, evaluation reports mask the overall results of change by highlighting specific events associated with it. For example, a report concerning computerization of the office will contain information about equipment purchase, training targets and deadlines for on-line performance. It should also include an overview of what the company wanted to achieve through computerization, how the action plan created opportunity for this achievement, where there were gaps between the spirit of the goal and what was actually achieved. Finally, what unexpected benefits or unnecessary mistakes occurred? And what are the recommendations about them?

This additional information requires an analysis of all pertinent facts surrounding the change. Report readers need this kind of analysis in order to decide whether the computerization was a success. Completion of training targets and a computer system which functions are certainly achievements. They fall far short of success if the original goal included a paper-free office, and staff still require paper back-up of files. In such a case, the computerization was a partial success only. A report which highlights the completion of specific goals rather than achievement of the desired change misleads the reader without intending to do so.

In-depth reporting   This is a suggested outline for an in-depth report:

1 *Project description*:
  • goals for change
  • rationale for these goals
2 *Summary of results*:
  • outline of the action plan
  • data gathered from action steps
  • description of methods used
  • any unplanned results and problems
3 *Contrast between goals and results*:
  • review of goals point by point against results
  • discussion of whether the symbol of success is achieved
4 *Recommendations for the future*:
  • benefits from the change
  • mistakes to be avoided in future
  • implications of the change

This format emphasizes a constructive criticism of the change rather than a summary of events and data. If readers challenge any recommendations, they open a debate that benefits the company. In contrast, when readers are not offered the essential points about a change, they are unable either to challenge or to provide support where it is needed.

Activity 13   *Please refer to the action plan developed in Activity 10 of the previous chapter (page 59) when answering the following questions.*

1 Do you want information about any specific activities? If so, what is it?
2 What purpose does this desired information serve (e.g. gain new insight, clarification of results, critique of the process, etc.)?
3 Who can give you this information?
4 Do you want to encourage a discussion or gather individual feedback? Why?

Writing questionnaires

This section is a guide for managers who want to survey the opinions and reactions of their colleagues. The written questionnaire is a time- and cost-saving way to do this. If questions are general enough, they can be used to evaluate other change projects as well. The questionnaire is a valuable tool for documenting reactions to change and gathering feedback about its effectiveness.

Some managers may hesitate to write their own survey questionnaires. They are familiar with published personality tests and industry-recognized attitude surveys. Producing their own for informal use can seem too great a task. Actually, many of these managers have worked with self-produced questionnaires during the whole of their careers. Whenever they interviewed a job applicant, they conducted an informal survey. Their purpose was discovery of information about the applicants, and they surveyed them to decide which applicant best matched the needs of the job.

The questions they chose were clear and precise so that applicants readily understood what information was asked of them. These interviewers avoided leading questions or the assumption that applicants have unlimited information about the company. For example, no manager would ask applicants to comment on the company cafeteria before they have actually experienced it.

When writing a questionnaire which surveys the results of change, common sense equally applies. Once the purpose for asking the questions is decided, specific issues are raised within questions which help to achieve that purpose. If information is needed from operators, in confidence, about the impact of a change on production, then questions emphasize production issues. If interest is in quality control, work flow, or management effectiveness, then questions address these topics. A clear objective for the questionnaire as a whole guides decisions about question areas and contributes to the overall clarity of the survey.

Having decided the purpose of the questionnaire, it is also necessary to decide how to administer it. A survey can be completed by a group of people together; this can encourage discussion. It can also be completed by separate individuals; this allows confidentiality. The choice is again guided by what purpose should be achieved through asking people questions. If the goal is to stimulate debate and increase the amount of feedback, then asking groups to complete a survey and then to discuss their answers together promotes this. Particularly when a change involves company reorganization, open questionnaire sessions with discussion lead to highly creative solutions and integration of the change. Alternatively, if individual reactions and personal response are desired then an anonymous or confidential questionnaire is the appropriate choice.

There are four choices for administration of surveys. They are:

- group completion with discussion
- anonymous: individual completion, unsigned
- confidential: individual completion, signed, with limited access to the results
- open: individual completion, signed, with general access to the results.

What to survey
The information which is needed to evaluate change may be obvious. If not, this can be decided by referring to the 'Monitoring' sections of the action plan (Activity 10, page 59). Are there any areas where monitoring of the change revealed ambiguous results? Were there any complaints or dissatisfaction expressed about the change? These should be closely examined because there may be information embedded in even unjust criticism.

Decide what result the implemented change should ideally have produced. Ask at least one question which ignores the actual results and instead focuses on what the respondent hoped would happen. This may uncover a hidden failing which wasn't immediately obvious to planners of the change. Ask if there is a quality or an atmosphere which was expected from the change. Another question can aim to discover the intangible results of the change in terms of personal reaction, for example: 'What word summarizes the atmosphere created by this change?' Other questions can include measurement of specific issues, such as time, preparation needs or expended resources.

These are topics which can guide the kinds of questions to be included in an evaluation survey:

- logged complaints from staff
- degree of disruption to routine
- ability to continue work
- training issues
- incidents of missing files, documents or equipment.

Gathering information about measurable incidents leads to discovery of deeper issues. For example, operators can reveal a lack of resources for the change even though management provided an adequate budget for overtime and equipment rental. This discrepancy needs further exploration. Was the company billed for equipment which didn't arrive? Were supervisors given warning about new schedule requirements? If not, where did communication break down? Did the finance department hold up payment of a deposit for an equipment rental so that it arrived too late to be of use? All of these issues highlight areas which can be improved for the next project. Each survey question not only gives information about the recently completed change effort, but also about organizational needs within the company.

Writing the questions
There are five main issues to consider when producing a questionnaire. They are: bias, wording, answer format, length, and sequence. Each of these issues is explained in detail here.

Bias

This refers to both the bias of the question writer as well as the bias of the survey participants. Writers' beliefs and attitudes influence the choice of questions as well as their wording. If these attitudes are positive, then a biased survey will offer questions which refer only to the beneficial aspects of the change. If attitudes towards the change are negative, then questions will emphasize mistakes or any inconvenient features. The ideal questionnaire gives participants an opportunity to give their views with minimum filtering through the views of the survey writer.

Participants also bring bias to questionnaires. They can interpret neutral questions as having a positive or a negative meaning, and even react angrily to what they have imagined. In some cases, being asked for an opinion is flattering enough to influence respondents to give positive answers. Also, if they know who or which team wrote the questionnaire, their personal feelings towards and relationships with those people can also influence their answers. This kind of bias is extremely difficult to address. At best, it can be minimized when the survey is given to a large number of participants. Extreme reactions within large groups tend to cancel each other out.

Suggestions:

- Test the questions first on colleagues who were not involved in the change.
- Check whether all the items reinforce the survey writer's own opinions about the change.
- Check whether the possibility of a negative or positive answer to any item makes the writer feel angry.
- If all items refer to factual matters, include some questions which ask for opinions and vice versa.
- Give the questionnaire to as great a number of people as is possible.
- Include a final question about the clarity of the questions and ask for comments about the survey in general.

Choice of words

The way in which questions are phrased is important. This section offers guidelines with examples for improving the wording of survey questions.

Guideline One:
Each item should refer to one incident or issue only.

Example: Were your opinions requested or your support sought for this change?

'Opinions' and 'support' may be related in the mind of the survey writer, but should be two separate questions within a survey. The words 'or' and 'and' are signals that there may be two topics included in one question.

Guideline Two:
Generalizations, ambiguous words and jargon should be avoided.

Example: please refer to the above sample question.

In this example, 'support' is an ambiguous term. It can refer to verbal encouragement as well as to the request to help carry boxes of equipment.

Guideline Three:
Leading questions produce confusing results. Items should avoid hinting at the desired answer or suggesting that the respondent agrees with certain beliefs or opinions.

Example: Were you able to implement this change fully because management was highly effective?

Alternatively, this could be two items:

• To what degree were you able to implement this change?
• Was management effective?

Guideline Four:
Another kind of leading question would be:

Example: Did contradictory messages lead to mistakes?

This question contains the assumption that contradictory messages were given. Alternatively, it should read:

• Were you given contradictory messages?
• If so, did they have an impact upon your performance?

Guideline Five:
Ask questions in a positive way.

Example: Was there too little time to implement change?

Negative questions confuse respondents. Alternatively, this first item should read:

• Was there enough time to implement this change?

Example: Did lack of preparation limit implementation?

Alternatively, this should read:

• What impact did preparation time have on your ability to implement the change?

Answer format
There are three kinds of answer formats which are useful when gathering information about change. These are answers which use: scales, either/ or, and open-ended responses. If more than one of these is included in

the questionnaire, care must be taken to avoid confusing or irritating participants by suddenly changing from one to the other. Questions which use the same kind of answer formats should be clustered.

Scales:
This format asks participants to measure their subjective responses to an item. It shows, in comparative terms, the degree or extent of their reactions to an issue. Commonly used scales are:

Example:	Agree very strongly	Agree	Undecided	Disagree	Disagree very strongly

Example:	Excellent		Average		Poor

Scales should not be varied within the questionnaire. Choose one kind of wording for measuring reactions and then stay with it for all the questions with scaled answers.

Either/Or:
This refers to 'true or false', multiple choice, and 'yes or no' types of answers. Although this is the most commonly used format, accuracy depends very much on the quality of the questions. An alternative answer can also be included, such as, 'sometimes' or 'doesn't apply'. The choices would read:

Example:	Yes	No	Sometimes
or			
Example:	Yes	No	Doesn't apply

Open-ended:
This format encourages comments from participants. It is particularly valuable when gathering information for a comprehensive review. Participants often volunteer information that otherwise would be missed. Unfortunately, open-ended answers take more time to read and summarize, especially if the answers are long and rambling.

To minimize this, use the open-ended answer format to supplement answers from either/or and scaled questions. For example, following a scaled answer, ask, 'Please comment'. Another way to give focus to open-ended answers is to phrase questions so that they refer to one point. 'What is your reaction to the new scheduling procedures?'

Length
An important issue is the length of the questionnaire. This decision should be based on the intended contents as well as the amount of time participants have to complete it. Here are some guidelines for planning this.

- Allow five minutes for respondents to read the directions.
- Allow one minute per question for multiple choice or true/false answers.

- Allow two or three minutes per item if written responses are requested.
- Allow five minutes for self-scoring surveys.

Thirty minutes is usually enough time for an evaluation questionnaire. This allows a mixture of approximately ten scales or either/or questions, and five open-ended ones. The setting for administering the survey is also a consideration. If there is privacy and quiet, this shortens the time participants need to settle down and concentrate. Also, it is more efficient to have the questionnaire and writing materials readily available to respondents as they arrive.

An important point is to recognize that surveys seek individual and personal responses to change. People generally consider their opinions and reactions to be their private property. They believe that they are doing the company a favour by giving them. A quiet setting and a ready supply of necessary materials shows courtesy and increases the likelihood that respondents will answer the survey fully.

Sequence

How questions are ordered can influence the quality of responses. General questions soliciting basic information should be at the beginning, and more challenging questions should follow. Also, questions asking about opinions and beliefs should go at the end. This allows participants to become comfortable with the process of answering the survey.

There should be a logical order to the questions so that they are easy to read. The function of a survey is to gather information. It is not intended to surprise people or show the writer's creativity. The sequence of questions should aid the participants' thinking process rather than challenge it.

Problem— analysis— discussion

Problem   A quality wool and sewing notions retailer enjoyed steady success during its 10-year period of operation. Based in the centre of an affluent town, its two owners found there was a high demand for their specialized goods and no real competition in the vicinity. The owners worked long hours, but paid themselves and their staff no more than average salaries. After purchasing the freehold of their premises, they gradually built up a substantial reserve and carefully invested it.

Six months previously, they decided to expand their business with a mail order service. Although they had no experience of that kind of operation, they were confident that their knowledge of quality knitting materials and their understanding of what their customers wanted would bring success.

Producing the first catalogue was a pleasure, and they had enough ready capital to finance a promotion campaign. Orders rapidly flowed in: some prepaid, but most on credit cards. The owners, delighted by this initial success, chose to expand the catalogue slightly and increase their mailing list. At the same time, a national newspaper approached them about using one of their knitting kits in a Sunday supplement promotion. Enthusiastically, they accepted.

In the weeks following the knitting kit promotion, they were inundated with requests. They also had orders as a result of their expanded catalogue, and a backlog from their original product line. Many customers chose to pay by credit card. For the first time, they lacked ready capital to purchase the wide range of necessary supplies. Their assets were in property and other non-liquid investments. They also lacked storage and work space as well as staff to make the kits, fill the orders and handle the paperwork. Their excitement changed to anxiety and stress as they struggled to organize their new ventures.

Analysis

Imagine that you are in the position of these retailers just as they are approached by the national newspaper. Please answer the following questions from that point of view.

1 What impact did the initial move to mail order sales have on the business in terms of:
   • products
   • facilities
   • people
   • markets
   • finance?
2 What were areas of weakness during the initial launch of the project?
3 What were areas of strength?
4 What specific aspect of success led to the decision to expand the business?
5 What steps can be taken to prepare for expanding the business further?

Discussion

These business owners illustrate some of the difficulties associated with rapid growth. Having expanded without preparation, they now must either borrow money to pay creditors and expand operations or else cash in some of their investments. Because they have a financially sound operation, this is possible and the crisis is a temporary one. If they continue this rapid growth, they should monitor their cash more carefully. Heavy investment in materials and a weakened cash position can be a disastrous combination if their sales suddenly drop.

They need to decide what they want to achieve through their business. Their personal and professional goals should be clearly described. Decisions about expansion should be based on their vision for the company. Growth for its own sake is unwise. Unless the owners are closet empire-builders, they will experience little satisfaction and great stress if they continue their current style of business expansion.

With a vision for the business, they can plan its growth. The decision to advertise knitting kits through a national newspaper is an excellent opportunity only if the owners are aware of the personal cost in terms of time and commitment. They can evaluate their company's growth periodically when they have created goals against which they can measure their achievement.

Summary

This chapter emphasizes the benefits of thoroughly evaluating change initiatives. This is both to determine the success of the change and also to discover organizational weaknesses revealed during the change. Standard company reports often do not allow inclusion of an individual's opinion about the results of the change. If the project's stated objectives are achieved, this can look like success. It is not if these objectives also create unforeseen problems or an undesirable overall result.

A recommended method for in-depth reporting is offered, with an outline which highlights the essential points. Also included in this chapter are instructions for producing questionnaires. The key features of question-writing are presented, with guidelines for avoiding bias.

Selected reading

Guba, Egon G. and Lincoln, Yvonna S., *Effective Evaluation*. San Francisco: Jossey-Bass, 1981.

Hamilton, David *et al.* (eds.) *Beyond the Numbers Game*. Basingstoke: Macmillan Education, 1977.

Perloff, Robert (ed.), *Evaluator Interventions: Pros and Cons*. London: Sage, 1979.

Smith, Nick L. (ed.), *New Techniques for Evaluation*. London: Sage, 1981.

6 Intelligent leadership

Leading change

In a homogeneous society where everyone shares the same background and values, mutual understanding is a common experience. Today's organizations are anything but homogeneous, and so an acceptance of differences is necessarily a feature of good management. This means that managers of change, particularly, need a flexible approach and demonstration of tolerance for their colleagues. Some leaders use a single style of leadership for all situations and all people, believing that this shows fairness to all. This approach actually limits leadership effectiveness. The manager's first task is to understand what different people need in terms of information and guidance and then offer this to them.

Intelligent leaders are self-aware. They recognize their own limitations and work consciously to balance their behaviour. This allows them to identify differences among their colleagues and to encourage cooperation based on that understanding. Change managed from this vantage point is likely to be more successful because these leaders help their colleagues to develop strengths and to manage weaknesses.

For many years the topic of leadership has been out of fashion. Keen supporters of consensus management have argued that designated leaders limit creativity and that intelligent people want to lead themselves. These ideas are in reaction to old-fashioned autocratic models of leadership and the gruesome abuses of power seen historically in world politics. Leadership at its best empowers others to express themselves. A leader provides focus and guides events so that colleagues are better able to contribute their best.

This is intelligent leadership, and intelligent groups of people welcome its presence. When managing change, this means taking responsibility for achieving a vision. It means presenting this vision in such a way that colleagues want to contribute to it and make it happen. This can only be accomplished with the exercise of a flexible attitude and skilled behaviour.

Case study

Infact Limited

> **The purpose of this case study is to illustrate the importance of discovering the best way to communicate with colleagues and clients. This manager identifies with other people's issues and ideas toward understanding them better and providing more effective leadership.**

Infact Limited is the world's best known independent trading floor consultancy and a leader in 'intelligent building' design. They work with information technology systems and facilities' layout to enhance a company's ability to conduct its business. Basing their designs on a thorough understanding of the organization, they meld its business needs with available technology. They listen carefully and then respond to needs for change. This, essentially, is intelligent leadership.

Paull Robathan, founder of Infact, suggests that leaders of change meet three criteria. They must want to understand the people and situations involved; have the right background in terms of ability, experience, and education; and be able to assess the situation fully from the clients' point of view. He says, 'To help me understand my client or my colleagues within the company, I need a sufficient background, a grounding in the things they are talking about. I actually have to understand them so well that I use their terms and assess the project from their perspective.' This adds up to *identifying with* them as well as *identifying what* they need.

This identification process requires more than data-gathering about the clients' new projects and company developments. Paull says, 'Not only do I work to know what clients want, but why they want it. Even when they describe what they need, it is my job to add value to this information and evaluate their needs from an informed and neutral point of view. I want to create a synthesis of what is needed with how it can be achieved.'

As an agent of change, Paull made his mark by speaking to a wide range of specialists in their own language: from traders to bankers to architects and to all the business professionals involved in a design project. 'It is a quintessential skill to be able to talk to people in their language. It means getting under their skin to discover the "hot buttons" for them: key words and key issues. But at the same time always staying neutral and advising from an outsider's perspective.'

He adds, 'At times, it's suggested that consultants by definition are biased. Those of us who sell brain power have to be very scrupulous and careful. This applies to change management because the client must believe that a change agent is neutral. There can be no hidden agendas for personal gain to the client's detriment.'

Change agents have enormous responsibility when guiding their projects and leading a decision-making process. Paull sums up his leadership role in this way: 'There is a paradox about what I do. The skills of convincing people to buy products that they don't want are exactly the same as those for selling them things that they do want. Identification with their real needs helps me avoid deluding myself and them about the relevance of what I offer them.'

Orientations to change: survey and analysis

A survey   A manager of change should assume that every individual on the change team or in the department responds differently to the same idea for change. Because many people contribute to the creation of a single change, they bring as many different backgrounds and attitudes to the task. As Paull Robathan suggests, a successful manager of change identifies with associates and clients in order to understand their needs and orientations to change. These leaders develop self-awareness about their own orientation and therefore work more effectively with their colleagues.

Although there are many attitudes to change, these can be organized into three main orientations. These are: initiators, planners and resisters. Initiators most often get the 'good press', while planners are considered somewhat calculating. Resisters are generally believed to be the most difficult people to manage. Each of these, it should be emphasized though, has both positive and negative aspects.

The following survey presents questions which lead to the discovery of orientation to change. It can also be used within a team as a catalyst for discussions about attitudes toward change. This added information about colleagues' orientations can be very helpful when working to implement change. Instructions for group use of this survey are provided in Activity 15 later in this chapter (page 99).

Directions
This survey provides 15 statements. Each of these is followed by three suggested choices. There are many other alternative courses of action, but please focus on these three and decide which action would be closest to an *initial response* to the statement.

Please score each choice from 1 to 3. A score of 3 shows greatest preference for one of the three choices. A score of 1 indicates least preference.

General statements

A You hear one of your management team say, 'I wish we could go back to the old days', and you:

1 privately agree   1 ____
2 feel annoyed by the lack of realism   2 ____
3 ignore the comment as impractical.   3 ____

B You believe by cutting expenditure immediately by 20 per cent overall, redundancies can be avoided; you decide to:

4 send key staff a memo announcing which cuts are essential   4 ____
5 decide to cut back temporarily on research and development effort   5 ____
6 review last year's budget figures to decide where to begin the cuts.   6 ____

C You win a prize for a luxury winter sports holiday and you have never ski'd. You:

7 ask for a cash equivalent prize instead of the holiday   7 ____
8 buy a learn-to-ski video and begin an exercise routine   8 ____
9 look forward to the first day of lessons.   9 ____

D Financial difficulties make you uncertain about the company's future, and so you:

10 review the last three years' figures to check trends   10 ____
11 remind the staff that they have gone through harder times   11 ____
12 explore ways to generate new income.   12 ____

E Increased competition has led to a significant loss of market share, and so you:

13 consider re-launching last year's successful product   13 ____
14 study competitors to discover their advantage   14 ____
15 completely review the business to discover problem sources.   15 ____

F When an important appointment is cancelled at the last minute, you feel:

16 thrown off course and annoyed about the wasted time   16 ____
17 relieved because you now have time to attend a different meeting   17 ____
18 grateful for an additional opportunity to prepare for tomorrow's activities.   18 ____

G When a project you are managing produces unexpected
and highly negative results, your *initial* response is:

19 to choose an action which will turn the results around   **19** ____
20 to implement damage control which preserves resources   **20** ____
21 to discover what went wrong.   **21** ____

H New technology requires redistribution of tasks and
responsibilities in your area, and so you:

22 display a flow chart which shows the new system and
announce its start date   **22** ____
23 assess individual skill levels toward creating a training
system   **23** ____
24 give half the staff new assignments and ask others
to continue former procedures.   **24** ____

I You have just been given responsibility for an important and
well-funded project. Your first response is to:

25 review all proposal documents and the budget   **25** ____
26 check the deadline feasibility   **26** ____
27 announce your aims and intentions to staff.   **27** ____

J You are offered the management of a 10-year project
that has no guarantee of success; you decide to:

28 tactfully decline the opportunity   **28** ____
29 accept and create evaluation phases at three-year
intervals which involve outside experts in project
assessment   **29** ____
30 commit to the project knowing that it is more likely
to take 15 years.   **30** ____

K You feel bored with your work and question whether your
career is going anywhere. You:

31 update your CV and explore the job market   **31** ____
32 decide to organize a new project   **32** ____
33 settle into the day's work because these moods pass.   **33** ____

Issues of risk
L You make an investment which drops sharply by 20 per
cent, the fall may be temporary. You decide to:

34 sell off your shares   **34** ____
35 confirm the company is solid and then hold on to the
shares   **35** ____
36 confirm the company is solid and buy additional shares.   **36** ____

M You inherit £60 000 unexpectedly; you:

37 buy the car of your dreams   **37** ____

38 put the whole amount into a building society account   **38** ____

39 take professional advice and invest it.   **39** ____

N You are offered a choice of three contracts and you choose:

40 a moderate salary with good benefits   **40** ____

41 a very generous commission on each unit managed,
moderate benefits, but no basic salary   **41** ____

42 a moderate commission on each unit managed, good
benefits, and a low basic salary.   **42** ____

O You have accumulated £10 000 prize money on a television
quiz show and can choose to stop there or double your
money with another question:

43 you take the £10 000   **43** ____

44 you choose the question because you are an expert on
this topic   **44** ____

45 you choose the question because you have a chance to
win £20 000.   **45** ____

Scoring instructions

Each of the 15 statements included in this survey has three possible
responses. Your choices represent an orientation toward change:
whether initiating, planning or resisting it.

Next to the space where you put your answers, there is a number in
bold type from 1 to 45. Refer to the three 'scoring columns' which follow
the examples offered below, and transfer your answers to a corresponding
numbered space in one of the columns.

Example

Your answers to the first statement may look like this:

1   3

2   1

3   2

Your answers to the second statement may look like this:

4   2

5   3

6   1

The numbers on the left each represent *one* of the possible answers to
the previous questions. The numbers on the right represent how likely
you are to pick that answer.

Sample scoring columns

Initiator		Planner		Resister	
2	1	3	2	1	3
5	3	6	1	4	2

Scoring columns

Initiator		Planner		Resister	
2	____	3	____	1	____
4	____	6	____	5	____
9	____	8	____	7	____
12	____	10	____	11	____
14	____	15	____	13	____
17	____	18	____	16	____
19	____	21	____	20	____
22	____	23	____	24	____
27	____	25	____	26	____
28	____	29	____	30	____
31	____	32	____	33	____
36	____	35	____	34	____
37	____	39	____	38	____
41	____	42	____	40	____
45	____	44	____	43	____

TOTALS   ____   ____   ____

When you finish, add the total score for each column (The three columns combined should total no more than 90.) Scores of equal numbers indicate a tendency to balance all three orientations to change. Your highest score shows your strongest bias. Your lowest score shows your area of least orientation.

An analysis All three areas are important when managing change, and awareness of orientation allows an improvement of overall performance. It is also important to ask: 'What are the orientations and preferences of colleagues and how can the team develop a more balanced approach?' When colleagues' orientations toward change are known, then the team can work more effectively together.

This allows them to play to each others' strengths. In a project team, initiators are best suited to break the ground by introducing the project to those outside the team or by discovering new features for the project. Resisters should be given tasks of risk management, or identifying potential problems. Planners should coordinate the project's detail. Regardless of preferences and orientations, the change must be implemented and so it makes sense to use all available team resources.

Recognizing the strengths and weaknesses of each orientation contributes to a successful completion of the project.

The three orientations are summarized here, followed by three profiles of managers. From the descriptions of their behaviour, their orientation to change may be obvious. Activity 14 helps analyse the information available about these managers as change agents.

The initiator
Sets ideas in motion. Is entrepreneurial and individualistic. Forgets the team in favour of energetic activity. Can be accused of insensitivity and callousness.

The planner
A steady performer. Thinks issues through and builds future ideas on past performance. Studies trends. Does not always consider implementation realities when deciding details. Can be accused of over-deliberation and inactivity or even ignorance of reality.

The resister
Conscientious and respectful of tradition. Wishes to retain the best of the past but is not always able to articulate this. Can be accused of negativity and an unwillingness to cooperate.

Profiles *Millicent Adams*
Within three years of Millicent's arrival in the marketing department as a researcher, she was appointed department manager. Again and again she identified trends and put information together to create exceptional marketing initiatives. She showed particular strength when thinking on her feet. Colleagues who knew when she was unprepared for meetings with senior executives were always surprised to learn that, once again, she convinced them to accept her ideas.

Although she was always affable enough, Millicent resisted developing friends in the department or even socializing with her colleagues. In fact, she once commented that office friendships seemed unprofessional to her. Only if a colleague were as ready as she to pool contacts and make new business connections, would she show real social skill and give attention to the relationship.

Colleagues with less drive viewed her as a human dynamo: impersonal, ambitious and entirely uncaring about anything other than work. But no one could deny that she was 'good news' for the department. Her performance and ideas reflected well on the whole team. Complaints arose only from those who wanted equal input into projects. Millicent tended not to recognize the value of other people's ideas. Her own were consistently successful, so why change?

Craig Edwards
All of Craig's immediate colleagues agreed that Craig was a very intelligent man and well placed in his role as New Projects Director in the research and development division. They also wondered at his ability to

carry so much exhaustive detail in his mind. His mental recall of past company performance and present circumstances allowed him to create impressive plans for the future.

Others had to rely on computers to organize information for complex projects. Craig could think through elaborate schemes, referring to his memory for detail and an understanding of industry trends. On paper, each action step would then be defined, organized and ready to go. Plans for product development and testing were masterpieces of orchestration.

His colleagues found him a little daunting because his super-organization skills tended to make average-level organizers look ill prepared. Actually, he readily assisted other team members in analysing planning issues so that overall he was a welcome and respected leader.

Criticism of his ability usually came from outside his area of expertise. Those who were required to implement his plans objected to his ignorance of production realities. Craig was often referred to as an 'ivory tower nutcase' by production managers charged with making prototypes of new products. Privately, one of these managers started to keep records of Craig's failures, toward requesting his eventual removal as New Projects Director.

Robert Hanson
Robert managed production for 25 years. He proved a loyal, dedicated company man and was recognized as such by his boss, the managing director. On many occasions, his understanding of production limitations saved the company time, money and valuable orders as he gave timely warnings to his boss about overtime, recruitment, and equipment renewal issues. This was his forte: to perceive warning signals *before* a crisis or problem developed.

In an industry generally rife with labour–management disputes, machine operators and their supervisors had only good things to say about Robert. While he pushed them to make quality goods with high efficiency, he always put their safety first. Add to this the basic respect he showed everyone, Robert was a much valued leader and boss.

His own colleagues among the plant management team and, in fact, the managing director, described him differently. They saw him as uncompromising, negative, slow-minded, and unwilling to change with the times. Although they believed him to be loyal to the company, he seemed so out of step with its current needs that this loyalty seemed valueless to them.

Robert, in turn, was ill at ease during the management group meetings and often avoided explaining his reasons for making demands on behalf of production. Actually, he felt unable to articulate these because his reactions were both intuitive and based on personal experience. Instead, he would automatically say 'no' to some new scheme from the 'hot shot' in marketing. Robert knew that eventually he would be overruled, but this ploy usually bought time for his department to catch up. Robert managed such sudden change for production by strategically dragging his feet in order to prepare for it properly.

Activity 14

1 Millicent Adams' orientation to change is:

2 Craig Edwards' orientation to change is:

3 Robert Hanson's orientation to change is:

4 Which of these managers seems most one-sided, which seems least?
5 If any one of these managers reported to you, what would you do to encourage them to improve their overall performance?
6 What is your own orientation to change and how can you improve your performance?
7 How can you improve your interaction with your colleagues when managing change?

Activity 15: for the group

The orientations to change survey is designed to encourage awareness that everyone reacts differently to change. The ability to accept and work creatively with these differences enhances a manager's ability to communicate, motivate and direct change efforts. The three orientations to change—initiator, planner and resister—lead to discussion about interpersonal issues. They emphasize that there is a need for balance and the inclusion of all three approaches when leading change.

It can be useful to suggest that all the members of a change team or all staff within the department take the survey together. The following activity provides instructions for leading this kind of session.

Materials
Copies of the survey, pencils, a quiet meeting place, a flipchart with paper, marker pens.

Instructions:

1 Distribute the survey and pencils, asking participants to complete the items.
2 Ask them to score the survey themselves when they get to the end.
3 If the group is larger than eight, form smaller groups of about five members. It may be tempting to lead groups larger than eight, but this will be a less productive exercise for the participants. Suggest that those who actually work together on a change project should join the same group.
4 On the flipchart, write:
   • what are your scores
   • one strength
   • one weakness.
5 Ask each group to choose a recorder, or if there is just one group, one member should volunteer to act as the recorder.

6 Each person should tell the group the scores for each orientation. Then give one strength which this orientation brings to the group. Finally, offer one weakness about this orientation which can be improved.

7 Each group should have approximately 10 minutes to discuss this. Many people dislike discussing their strengths and weaknesses. Recorders should encourage discussion while avoiding an over-directive manner.

8 Recorders should report a summary to the whole group of:
   • number of members having each orientation
   • strengths the group brings to the change
   • weaknesses the group wants to improve.

9 If there is only one group, then all of its members can summarize together.

Delegation

After recognizing and accepting different orientations to change, the task is to draw these together to achieve a common purpose. Widespread company change must engage the energy and attention of every employee if it is to succeed. One way to achieve this is through effective delegation of responsibility and sharing of authority for making the change happen. This is both an art and a method.

Many managers learn delegation skills in the hit or miss college of business. Their method is a blend of common sense and experience. Sometimes it works and sometimes it doesn't. They would like a systematic approach, but are far too busy to search for it. It is common for managers to think that they are delegating successfully, only to receive criticism later that they don't delegate enough.

When delegating, another person is given the power to decide how to complete a task. Projects that require extensive instruction and constant supervision are either unsuited to delegation or are assigned to the wrong people. Once the desired result is described and guidelines and back-up information are provided, supervision must occur at a distance. If it doesn't, then this is interference, not delegation.

The major responsibility when managing change is to monitor the delegatees' progress and be available to give them support and advice. By watching from a distance, the manager can also discover the effects of change on other parts of the project. As staff carry out their delegated tasks, they in turn delegate. This second level of delegation needs supervision as well. If a manager is too involved in supervising the details of the project, then there won't be the time or the perspective to oversee the whole process of change.

Delegation is also an excellent means for building a team. Colleagues feel trusted and respected when they are delegated appropriate tasks. It is a risk to leave details to colleagues, but it is a calculated one. The likelihood of error is minimized when tasks are matched to the skills and abilities of people.

Although there is a great deal written about delegation, much of this emphasizes concepts and explanations about why delegation is necessary for management efficiency. Managers need a practical approach. Effective delegation includes four essential points which are readily applicable to work situations. This section presents a step-by-step approach to delegation, with an explanation for each step within the process.

These are the four steps for successful delegation:

- Define the task
- Present the reason for its importance
- Explain any expectations
- Monitor and evaluate progress.

Define the task   Because this step is so obvious, it is often given the least attention, particularly if there are clear goals for change. In delegation, the limits of each specific task still need to be outlined. Ideas for this can emerge from delegatees as the manager asks them how best to complete the task. Those who are delegated responsibility feel empowered when they have helped decide what a job should include. This decision should then be summarized into a few written sentences, with copies kept by the manager as well as the delegatee. Any changes to the assignment would then be added to these notes. This not only provides a basis for performance evaluation, but also contributes valuable information to a final project report. This process is often called 'creating ownership'. Good delegators encourage people to feel responsible for the success of their work so that they 'own' its achievement themselves.

Present the reason for its importance   'Possessive ownership' is avoided when time is also taken to explain the reason for the task. This means describing how the task contributes to other assignments, to the project itself and to the whole company. Giving the 'big picture' encourages understanding, interest and involvement. The junior people on the team appreciate this most. It is a sign that the boss takes them seriously and wants them to understand the importance of their job. This explanation is best given when they are first assigned the task because it may influence any suggestions they offer toward creating a job definition.

Explain any expectations   This step includes describing the kind and amount of responsibility delegatees are given to complete the task. The limits of their authority should be explained as well as the circumstances under which they should seek advice before decision-making. This implies that they are also told when, where and how they can reach an adviser for this support. Delegators create serious problems, if not crises, when they delegate and then simply disappear. This is the opposite of over-supervision.

Although a different problem, it is equally frustrating to be on the receiving end. It also seriously jeopardizes the success of the project.

Delegatees want clear performance standards and information about how the task will be evaluated. This removes ambiguity, a major cause of stress at work. If questions are encouraged at the beginning of the task, answers clarify what successful completion looks like for this assignment.

Monitor and evaluate progress

This step refers to the leader's ultimate responsibility for the completed task. If progress is monitored effectively, there is a double yield: the work is done and also the delegatee has a sense of achievement, with minimal risk to the project's success. If expectations have been explained in advance, then the harsh edge of criticism is removed at the project's completion.

When delegatees know their requirements in advance and actually help to define them, there is a sense of fairness in the evaluation. When the task's outcome is discussed in terms of prearranged targets, delegatees can be given direct feedback without morale loss, hurt feelings or complaint. This is a critique of a specific performance, not of the person.

It is also important to give recognition where it is due. Even when there have been weak areas, find at least one strength and say this aloud. Too often managers say, 'They know what they did well. I don't need to say so.' This is a mistaken view. Positive feedback is one way to reassure colleagues. It also offers them an example of the kind of performance that is valued. When they have clear performance standards, they can choose to modify their behaviour to meet them.

Leadership dilemma

Even good leaders can be criticized for ignoring their colleagues' advice and comments. The real issue often has little to do with their willingness to listen or their openness to feedback. Instead, leaders under pressure may *hear* what is said, but then are unable to fit this information into their own understanding of the situation. When they cannot make sense of the offered comments or information, they often discount it. This problem is far more serious than simply ignoring their colleagues' comments. It is related to the leaders' ability to be curious, to think creatively and to interpret information in a positive way.

Making an assumption that there is meaning in what a colleague says adds a dimension to the management of change. Rather than discount a comment as meaningless, a manager should ask, 'What does this person intend to say? Have I missed some vital point?' This is difficult when the remarks seem time-wasting, negative or just plain stupid. This approach marks a return to the discussion about framing and reframing in Chapter 3 (page 40).

Surprising results come about when attentive listening and creative thinking are added to leadership style. The assumption that each contribution to the team is a meaningful one—even if its value is not immediately obvious—shows profound respect. Colleagues not only experience the respect, but this positive style will be infectious. A work atmosphere which assumes the best fulfils this prophecy.

Lateral and vertical thinking

In the 1960s, Edward de Bono proposed that there are two distinctly different kinds of thinking. He called the two 'vertical' and 'lateral', and suggested that managers could increase their effectiveness by learning to use both kinds. The two approaches relate to Chapter 4's discussion about right and left brain thinking in the section 'Symbol of Success' (page 64), and produce two very different styles of communication.

Vertical thinking is analytical. It is a tendency to focus on how the separate parts of an idea fit together. Solutions to problems are created by discovering which part doesn't fit or what is missing from the idea. Vertical thinkers get new ideas often by dismantling and reorganizing old ones. They are skilled mental recyclers. Their creativity is based on an ability to work logically and sequentially through any problem.

Lateral thinking is intuitive. It is a tendency to let an idea emerge by studying a number of separate possibilities. Solutions to problems are created by discovering ways to relate these separate possibilities together. This involves discarding some possibilities and redefining others in the quest for some new thinking arrangement and a solution to the problem. Lateral thinkers get new ideas by finding new relationships for a set of individual parts. They are often called visionary because they describe an idea in terms of a complete whole.

Lateral and vertical thinkers emphasize different features of a project or idea. They describe things in very different ways. For example:

Lateral: 'By the new year we will have a tower ready for use as a lighthouse. The right materials will be used and work accomplished efficiently as a team effort.'

Vertical: 'By 1 January, we will build a lighthouse. Our team will fit 20 000 bricks together and install a high-power lighting system so that it will be ready for use.'

When these two kinds of thinkers work together without awareness of their basic differences, they can create serious misunderstandings. The tendency to emphasize different aspects of a problem or prioritize different features during discussion can lead to repeated arguments. Debate doesn't seem to resolve differences. This is because the debaters don't realize that they often discuss completely different problems, using the same terminology but giving the words a different significance.

For example, a vertical thinker will read this chapter in sequence before considering its merits and deficiencies. A lateral thinker will dip in and out of the sections deciding which parts have something relevant to offer. When these different-thinking individuals meet on a change management team, verticals suggest that laterals are superficial, imprecise and careless. Laterals describe verticals as slow-thinking, overly cautious and weighed down by detail.

Laterals can readily describe how a completed project will look, but may miss vital deadlines. Verticals can set stages to reach the goal, but may not include aspects of the task essential for its successful completion. Both analytical and intuitive orientations are necessary for a successful team. Every team member needs to be conscious of the possibility of such basic differences so that they avoid unnecessary conflict. Recognition of different approaches allows the team to gain benefit from both styles.

Building the team

Delegation contributes to the sense of team because it empowers colleagues, encourages their participation and shares the excitement of achieving change. It allows leaders to express awareness of their own limitations and their dependence on the team for success. Rather than undermine their authority as leaders, this actually enhances it. When staff are given the responsibility of completing work as well as clear explanations about how the work will be monitored, this actually increases the leaders' standing within the team. It is a paradox in groups that the more power a leader gives away as an effective delegator, the more respect and influence he or she actually gains.

Teams need clear guidelines and a leader's willingness to express authority on behalf of the company. It is very difficult to work for 'nice guy bosses' who never make clear what they want. These leaders argue that the team should lead itself or that team members should take charge as needed. In fact, this behaviour leaves their team-mates without a standard bearer, a spokesperson, a guide, a champion or any of the other vital roles a team leader plays.

These nice guys are difficult to challenge because negative remarks will seem ungrateful, or even critical of their niceness. A good leader does the team a favour by expressing clearly which decisions belong to the leader and which belong to the team. When this is openly and non-emotionally stated, team members can challenge the leader freely and debate the issue of authority openly. Genuinely nice guys encourage this behaviour and earn far more respect from their team than by avoiding the power issue entirely.

The Brown model

Leaders who want to develop a sense of team can benefit from the observations of George Brown who conducted research during the mid-eighties at the University of California. He suggests that there are phases which groups experience as they create the elusive quality of 'team spirit'.

These phases are:

- Awareness of self
- Awareness of others
- Appreciation of differences
- Contact
- Trust
- Respect
- Sense of team

Many team-building models suggest that teams are based on trust. In these models, leaders are advised to build trust and then a sense of team will follow. This leaves unanswered the question: How do you build trust? This is particularly challenging when a manager is expected to lead a group which has a history of internal conflict.

The Brown model suggests that three additional phases contribute to the development of trust. Leaders who want to establish a trusting atmosphere within the group should start by encouraging the group's individual members to increase their self-awareness. This means they should examine their own patterns of behaviour within the group toward better understanding their motivation. Honest self-assessment leads to increased awareness about the impact which their behaviour has on other group members. As soon as individuals see the potency of their own actions, they become more aware of other members of the team.

A lack of awareness can lock individuals into blaming behaviour, self-justification and judgemental posing. From this perspective, problems and conflicts really do seem to be entirely the other person's fault. Self-awareness changes this. It allows group members to observe how they interact with their colleagues.

In this process, they also begin to recognize that their colleagues are truly different from them. Intellectually, they know this already. Obviously, their colleagues are different in terms of motives, needs, backgrounds, behaviour and so on. In practice, much conflict results from the blind belief that people share a common understanding of a situation and a common reason for their behaviour.

Awareness of self

Here is a simple example. Bob accuses Henrik of stealing supplies. In fact, Henrik, a new transfer to the department, does not know that he should sign a request form whenever he takes office supplies. Bob lacks awareness that his blaming behaviour is not only unpleasant for Henrik, but entirely unjustified.

Awareness of others

He also doesn't realize that his colleagues in general profoundly dislike him. He is locked in a state of unawareness, where he continues to blame, judge and accuse others, never fully realizing the impact this has on other people.

Appreciation of differences

If he is given an opportunity to discover more about himself, he can become aware of the reactions to his behaviour. He recognizes that Henrik's behaviour is motivated by ignorance, not deceit. Once this occurs, he can begin to explore how different other people are from himself. He is free to like them or leave them based on who they really are, rather than who he thinks they are. This is the recognition, the acceptance and the appreciation of differences.

Contact

When group members are self-aware and can appreciate that others have the right to be different, then genuine contact can occur. This is person-to-person, eyeball-to-eyeball communication. Much interaction in working life is mask-to-mask or posture-to-posture. This superficial and self-protective behaviour may actually be justified in highly competitive and individualistic environments. It is self-defeating in a team.

Trust

Contact occurs when individuals are self-aware enough to see and hear their colleagues as different individuals. Contact creates good relationships, enthusiasm and productive ideas. Inevitably it also leads to the development of trust. If enough time and attention has been given to the first three phases of team-building, then trust grows.

Respect

It is respect that inspires group members to willingly identify each other as team-mates. Trust alone doesn't create a team bond. This occurs when team members value their association with each other. The presence of respect turns a group of associates into a team.

Sense of team

The memories of good teams linger on long after the team experience is over. The quality of mutual acceptance found in a team enhances the enjoyment of each other's company and leads to greater productivity. Team-work is a value to the company, but rushing the formation of teams is a mistake. This is particularly so when managing change.

Team development

Figure 6.1 offers a model for the development of a sense of team. Self-awareness leads to an awareness of others and an appreciation of differences which then creates contact. On the flow diagram, 'contact' is followed by a 'yes' or 'no'. When group members experience contact, this is a 'yes'. They then move to the next phase of team development, trust.

If team leaders believe the group lacks trust, this is a signal that its members should return to the first phase, development of self-awareness. Telling group members to be more trusting often has the opposite effect. Instead, it is best to encourage group members to discover more about their own behaviour within the group and then to improve their acceptance of the other team members' individual differences.

Whenever a lack of trust is indicated, this is the most effective solution. It is time-consuming, but that is the nature of team-building. Teams are never finished. As a team's members grow and change, team leaders must continually find ways to renew the sense of team. They can achieve this by providing team members with opportunities to discover positive aspects about their colleagues, to accept the negatives and to remind them of the bond which their mutual trust creates.

When trust is achieved, then the team begins to experience mutual respect. Team spirit is inspired when members remind each other of this shared respect. This in turn leads to a sense of team. On the diagram, there are arrows leading from a 'sense of team' to 'yes' or 'no' answers. Leaders who want to further develop or renew team spirit can periodically return to the trust-building phase of team-building or to the initial phase of developing self-awareness.

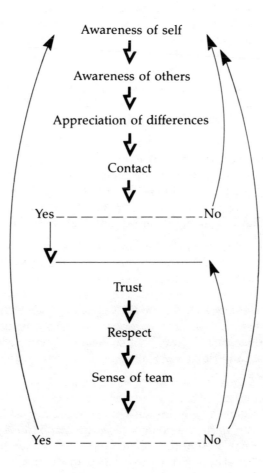

Figure 6.1 The Brown model for team-building

Problem—
analysis—
discussion

Problem   The Chairman of the Board and Chief Executive Officer of a pharma-
ceuticals company with world-wide markets is well known within the
company for his political skills. It is generally accepted that people and
proposals which the chairman doesn't like don't go very far, despite
their merit or value to the company. 'Survivors' know that their wisest
course of action is to seek the chairman's approval for new ideas privately before going public with them. This saves time, loss of face and
wasted effort in the long run.

The director of marketing in this company is a woman in her early
forties. She was head-hunted from the soap industry five years before
and weathered successfully the company insiders' double bias against
her gender and her background in 'washing-up liquid'. In fact, she
gained much respect as her market campaigns steadily increased the
company's market share and enhanced its image. It has been her private
ambition, though, to move from marketing to operations and eventually
to the CEO's position on his retirement. None of her co-directors seem
aware of this. They include her in 'company leadership' gossip as if she
were a precocious child rather than a potential rival.

The politically sharp chairman does recognize her ambition and decides
to use this to his own advantage. His goal is to ensure her continued
marketing effort in the company while satisfying her need for status. To
this end, he includes her in the weekly briefing sessions he has with the
operations director who is also nearing retirement. This tactic is to
imply his support for her advancement while promising her nothing.

Keen to learn all she can from these company leaders, she also begins
to meet even more regularly with the operations director. Gradually,
she assumes informal responsibility for one of his operations initiatives.
Peace seems to reign as the president privately continues to groom his
own candidate for the CEO position. Then without warning, the marketing
director visits the chairman and resigns. Because her position is so sensitive, she suggests that she leave immediately and adds that she has
already cleared her office.

When asked for an explanation, she answers that the company's main
competitor has invited her to be their vice president of operations. They
base their selection on her advanced degree in biochemistry, her 15
years of management within the soap industry, and her past five years
in her present post. Given the multi-million budget she will manage,
she believes that the rival company offers her a better career opportunity.
She adds that most of her present staff intend to resign as well and
move to new positions under her. Enraged, the chairman calls security
to have her escorted from the building.

Analysis
1 What is the chairman's blind spot?
2 What is his orientation to change?
3 What is the marketing director's orientation to change?
4 What feature(s) of delegation were lacking when the chairman included the marketing director in the weekly operations meetings?
5 If this marketing director reported to you for the duration of a change project, how would you encourage her best performance?

Discussion
There is a major difficulty for managers who depend solely on manipulation and political skill for leadership influence: no one trusts them. The more friendly and helpful they behave, the more carefully their colleagues search for an ulterior motive. Also, long-term success with office politics tends to create complacency and the naive belief that this success will continue unchallenged.

Any manager, male or female, who at the age of 40 reaches the level of this marketing director is a force to be taken seriously. The chairman calculated what she would do according to an outdated idea that director-level managers remain with the same company until retirement. He also was unable to imagine how angry she would feel about his manipulation and how coolly she would respond.

During her first two years as marketing director, she realized that an upward move within this company would be almost impossible. During the last three years she stayed to meet the challenge of succeeding with all the odds against her. She also decided to gain needed experience before moving to another director-level post. The decision to move actually resulted from the chairman's decision to include her in the weekly meetings with the operations director. This gave her the necessary exposure to high-level operations issues.

If the chairman studied his colleagues more realistically, he would have recognized her potential value to the competition. This would have led to a more serious effort to keep her in the company rather than a mismanaged trick to gain her compliance. The moral of the story is this: desirable people are also sought by other leaders. It is wisest to treat them well.

Summary

This chapter emphasizes the importance of intelligent leadership. This means a flexible management style which is based on self-awareness and which empowers others to perform at their best. A personality survey, 'Orientations to change', highlights three different personality approaches to change, that of the resister, the planner and the initiator. Managers can use the survey to create a discussion among their colleagues toward recognizing and accepting their different orientations.

Another section outlines four points for successful delegation. These are: define the task, present the rationale, explain expectations, and monitor results. The communication challenges of managing change are also discussed. Managers are asked to recognize whether they are vertical or lateral communicators, that is, intuitive or analytical. The importance of becoming aware of differences leads to the section on team-building, with a model offered to guide this vital process.

Selected reading

Argyle, M. (ed.), *Social Skills and Work*. London: Methuen, 1981.

Bennis, Warren and Nanus, Burt, *Leaders: The Strategies for Taking Charge*. New York: Harper & Row, 1985.

Block, Peter, *The Empowered Manager*. San Francisco: Jossey-Bass, 1987.

Burn, James M., *Leadership*. New York: Harper & Row, 1978.

de Bono, Edward, *Lateral Thinking for Management*. New York: Penguin, 1982.

de Bono, Edward, *The Mechanism of Mind*. London: Penguin, 1990.

Eisenberg, Eric M. and Witten, Marsha G., 'Reconsidering Openness in Organizational Communication', *Academy of Management Review*, **12**, 3, 1987, 418–426.

Halperin, Samuel, *A Guide for the Powerless and Those Who Do Not Know Their Own Power*. Washington DC: Institute for Educational Leadership, 1981.

Handy, Charles, *Understanding Organizations*. London: Penguin, 1985.

Kanter, Rosebeth Moss, *The Change Masters: Corporate Entrepreneurs at Work*. London: Allen & Unwin, 1985.

London, Manuel, *Change Agents: New Roles and Innovation Strategies for Human Resource Professionals*. San Francisco: Jossey-Bass, 1988.

March , J. and Olsen, J., *Ambiguity and Choice in Organizations*. Bergen, Norway: Universitetsforlaget, 1979.

Merry, Uri and Brown, George I., *Neurotic Behavior of Organizations*. Cleveland, OH: Gardner, 1986.

Smith, Kenneth and Berg, David, *Paradoxes in Group Life*. San Francisco: Jossey-Bass, 1987.

7 Resistance—the repercussions of change

What is resistance? Resistance at its most obvious is a slow-motion response to meet agreements or even a complete refusal to cooperate with change. In an organization, resistance is opposition or withholding of support for specific plans or ideas. It can be either intentional or unintentional, covert or overt.

Leaders who are self-aware and have a sense of humour have the best chance of success when managing resistance. Unfortunately, those who lack these essential qualities also lack the means to acquire them, that is, awareness and a sense of humour. This is a vicious circle with an ironic end-result. Those who are flexible and adaptable themselves are able to deal effectively with resistance. Those who are not have difficulty, and they even provoke further resistance as they attempt to force change. This chapter is for these managers as well as for those who already manage resistance with skill. The techniques offered are generic and apply to a wide variety of situations.

One of the great difficulties about managing resistance is the need to avoid inadvertently creating resistant situations. Often, those who resist change refuse more forcefully when they see others around them supporting it enthusiastically. This issue is a challenge for managers of change. It far outweighs any other aspect of the change process, whether this is goal-setting, understanding company needs, planning and implementation, evaluation or leadership issues.

This is because resistance can seem irrational and develop without warning, interrupting any activity at any time. The choice to ignore its first minor appearance can lead to trouble later, and yet an overly firm reaction to trivial incidents of resistance can make a manager look like a bully. Resistance is a way to say 'no' to change. Wisely used, this is a valuable contribution to the change process. Randomly or irresponsibly employed, it causes unbearable stress and considerable bad feeling.

It is the managers' task to work creatively and rationally with resistance. As effective leaders, they cannot afford to ignore their colleagues when they disagree with change because even annoying instances of resistance can be based on sound thinking and realism. When everyone within an organization responds to change easily, then this is as fortunate as the situation is unusual. Age, background, learning style and work habits contribute to differing responses to change.

Other difficulties arise when there is a basic misunderstanding or lack of agreement about what needs to change. This problem is particularly damaging because these disagreements can develop *after* all the plans are made as well as before. Managers who assume that they have company-wide support for a proposed change can resent the discovery of unexpected resistance to what they believe is a wholly beneficial idea.

Management challenge

The management challenge is complex. First, resistance must be discovered. Occasionally, resisters themselves don't realize that they are withholding support. This commonly occurs when staff receive poor communication about what is expected of them. It is an easy solution for senior managers to blame the machine operator, delivery agent or clerical staff for an inability to respond to change. Discovering precisely *who* is resisting and *why* is the real task when managing change. A signal that change is mismanaged from the top is repeated evidence that an entire department, group or team fails to implement change correctly. Either their manager has not understood the requirements or has chosen to resist the change while verbally agreeing to it.

The second feature of this challenge is the need for a balanced approach. Leaders must avoid any over-reaction to resistance once it is discovered. Realistically, a manager should recognize that every change creates some resistance and expect it to emerge at every stage of a change process. All plans for change should include an awareness of this possibility. Rather than resent resistance, leaders should assume that negative reactions can lead to constructive information about the change. By entering into non-emotional debate with resistors, they can discover ways to improve the change project.

Making resistance 'normal' leads to discussion which stimulates change rather than threatens it. The best and least expensive way to deal with resistance is to encourage expression of differing opinions toward reaching a common understanding of the problem. Although comments from resistors are often initially critical, even forcefully so, this is just one step in the process of resolving the issues which they raise.

Leaders should encourage group members to give feedback and contribute ideas: both positive and negative. Managers of change can only benefit from these comments. The task is to listen and, where necessary, guide colleagues to reframe their negative or hostile responses. An open-minded attitude and free debate actually minimize resistance even though comments and reactions to change sound negative and even destructive.

Some managers react forcefully to resistance. Their aim is to control it; stop it; negate it; in short, make it go away. This response doesn't work because it *resists* resistance. It is a defensive reaction to a defensive action. It creates two entrenched and resistant positions, not just one, with neither side willing to give way to the other.

Those who resist plans for change may in fact have different definitions of the problem or beliefs about its seriousness. While they may say aloud that, 'This plan won't work', they may actually be thinking, 'This plan doesn't address the real issue.' Only through discussion can mutual understanding be developed.

To resolve resistance, a manager must willingly explore what causes it. There is no other way. Acknowledging contradiction and criticism can seem like playing into the hands of the opposition. This is where both self-awareness and a sense of humour bring most benefit. Managers with a balanced and fair perspective and the ability to maintain a 'light touch' are always in control. This is because for them 'control' includes the idea that other people can have different points of view. Managers control change by coordinating these differences into an integrated whole and by allowing colleagues to contribute their positive and negative views.

At times, leading change leaves managers open to personal attack. They need to remember that the criticism is directed toward the change, not the person managing it. A sense of humour helps managers avoid taking themselves too seriously. This, in itself, is a powerful antidote to resistance. It is difficult for a colleague to feel coerced by a manager who encourages discussion and a light-hearted approach.

Activity 16
1 What is your *emotional* response to a colleague saying 'no' to you (this does not refer to rational, reasonable or intelligent responses)?
2 If this varies from colleague to colleague, what influences your response?
   • your relationship to the person?
   • their status in the company?
   • their courtesy?
   • their intelligence?
   • another reason?
3 How do you monitor your emotional biases when colleagues say 'no'?
4 Is there anyone you admire who manages resistance extremely well?
5 What do you admire about them?

Case study

> **The purpose of this case study is to illustrate the importance of a flexible attitude when managing resistance to change. The leader involved creates a positive climate for innovation by providing information about new ideas and encouraging their discussion throughout the company. This, employee commitment, and skilled management resolve resistance as it occurs.**

Seymour Duncan Research is a California-based firm which designs and manufactures consumer electronic products for the music industry. Cathy Carter Duncan, the company's Chief Executive Officer, maintains a positive attitude toward change, particularly when managing resistance. She says, 'I believe that flexibility for change is a prerequisite in today's business environment. There are always going to be changes from internal and external forces, and it's necessary to know how to deal with this. The only constant for our company is the fact that things are constantly changing. All the best companies listen to the market, their employees, and then make changes. This takes more energy, but we can and will do it. This flexible attitude throughout the company saves us a great deal of resistance.'

Cathy also adds that a service attitude is another antidote to resistance. 'Change is easy if you have communication and a concept of service between departments. Each smaller team in an organization can resist change, especially if the change is initiated by a different department. If there is a service orientation throughout the company, then the departments work to help each other. Every employee belongs to a small group, but they want to service the larger group, the whole company, too. This comes ultimately from wanting to offer the customer continually improving service and goes beyond just giving a big smile to the outside world.'

One of the ways in which Cathy creates a culture for change is through a strong communication network within the company. 'Any time there are significant changes in an organization, especially in the restructuring you see today, people can get nervous and feel concerned. You need to address these issues because they have a negative impact on performance. Communication is the key. In our company we have an "open door policy" where any employee can come to any manager's door, including my own, whenever they choose.

'We also have monthly company-wide meetings where we update everyone on the state of the economy, business sales, and areas for quality improvement. On alternate months we divide into two groups, production people and paper people, for educational events, problem-solving and other issues.' These meetings serve as a vehicle for regular communication and ensure that everyone in the company operates on the same wavelength and toward the same goals.

One result of open communication is the creative p
within the Seymour Duncan management team. E
suggestions for improvements or new directions fo
highly creative process includes the whole team ge
together. These are written on flipchart paper and h
Then everyone analyses each suggestion. This provi
points of view and an opportunity for frank discussio
ences of opinion still exist, the team continues to analy
until the right one becomes obvious.

If it emerges that key individuals offer strong resistance to a project after it has been decided, Cathy is willing to ask the team to go back and reconsider the decision. This is expensive management time, but she considers it essential to ensure that the team acts together. At times, it isn't immediately obvious *who* is resisting the change. Everyone appears to agree, but the change isn't implemented. Only through open and honest discussion can they discover what holds back commitment to the change.

'It is worth while taking that extra time to re-assess the problem. We may be wrong. This person may be right. We have to listen to this.' While Cathy is willing to make the decision to let go those people who resist necessary change, she weighs that decision very carefully. Seymour Duncan's human resources are key to the company's success. As CEO, she may decide to drop the idea rather than the person.

'Resistance is emotionally fatiguing and financially burdensome. Having a flexible attitude is like having insurance. What sane business person wouldn't have insurance or wouldn't build an environment of flexibility to change? It's the sensible approach. You're looking for trouble otherwise.'

The discovery process

When managing resistance, the first step is to recognize when it occurs. Sometimes this discovery begins with an intuition that something is not right. At other times, resistance is more obvious. As Cathy Carter Duncan described, she may hear that everyone agrees to the change, but then nothing happens. This is a form of resistance.

Having recognized resistance, managers need a strategy for resolving it. Resolution depends on how skilfully they proceed. Suggesting that self-awareness and a sense of humour are antidotes for resistance can seem less useful to a manager whose entire staff have just walked off the shop floor. Even so, these qualities are very important. They contribute to the mental flexibility required for facing this kind of situation. They are qualities which prevent blind, and even stupid, reactions to colleagues who say 'no' to change.

This is an important point, particularly when members of a team are all equally senior within the company. Professional partnerships, company boards, trustees or managers seconded to project teams illustrate situations where tact is required to deal with resistance. Flexibility *allows* flexibility. Even a firm management style should include the possibility of assessing each case of resistance on its own merits. A single response to all situations of resistance is unlikely to prove a successful tactic. Instead, a strategic approach benefits resistance management. This can be developed from two different sources of information.

The first of these analyses each instance of resistance to discover *categories of behaviour*. With this information, managers can explore the motivation of the resisters and better decide a response to them and the issues which they raise. The second source of information explores possible *causes of resistance*. Understanding the basic cause of resistance can guide the discussion of issues and problems associated with the change. This would focus specifically on why there is resistance and leads to decisions about the appropriate response to it.

The following two sections present techniques for developing these two sources of information. The matrix offered in the next section, 'Categories of behaviour', provides a tool for organizing information about resistance. Four categories of resistant behaviour are offered. The section following this, 'Causes of resistance', directs attention to *why* resistance has occurred. There are five diagnostic questions which managers can use to discover the source of resistance. When the source of resistance is revealed, then colleagues' concerns about the change can be more easily addressed.

Categories of behaviour: a matrix

When evidence of resistance first appears, it helps to examine this in terms of *how* it has been expressed. Is the resistance overt or covert? Also, have resisters been conscious or unconscious that their behaviour has undermined change? These two extremes—overt versus covert and unconscious versus conscious—provide a means to categorize behaviour. Recognizing categories of resistance allows a manager to choose a course of action more effectively.

Covert and overt

Resistance can be covert so that lack of support for change is either concealed or undefined. It can also be overt so that those who resist change express their point of view openly and offer their reasons for disagreement. Although overt resistance leads to debate, and on occasion conflict, it is easier to manage than covert resistance. In cases of overt resistance, managers can see and hear their adversaries. This allows them to work directly with the situation toward resolving it.

Those who resist change covertly can often completely avoid detection. An extreme political example includes the spy. In business, covert resisters are often ambitious colleagues who carefully undermine projects which give a reward to their rivals. They operate secretly in order to protect their own interests. Managers of change experience this form of resistance as a serious challenge because they often don't discover it until it is too late.

Unconscious and conscious

There are two other extremes of behaviour. These refer to the motivation for resistance. This can be either unconscious or conscious. When resistance is unconsciously motivated, colleagues do not actually realize that their behaviour undermines the change. In this case, their actions are based on wrong information, poor training or deeply ingrained habits from previously set work routines. Alternatively, they may realize that their behaviour doesn't always match newly assigned requirements, but they rationalize their occasional return to old habits as 'doing the company no real harm'.

Unconscious resistance creates management difficulty because the resisters believe themselves to be entirely innocent of 'resistance'. They are doing their job, not resisting change. Those responsible for the new project can seem highly over-reactive if they express anger about a lack of cooperation which is based on unconscious motives. This response contributes to poor morale and only succeeds in generating bad feeling.

Resistance which is consciously motivated is also a serious challenge. These resisters adopt their position after considering the change. They may be misinformed, or even self-serving, but their opinions must be heard. If they are not, then their resistance only increases. Entering into debate serves the change.

Double matrix

These four extremes of resistance can be presented as a double matrix.

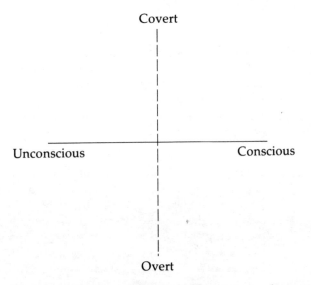

This matrix forms quadrants which categorize four extremes of behaviour. Each of these defines four readily identifiable kinds of resistance. These are:

- Covert and conscious
- Covert and unconscious
- Overt and unconscious
- Overt and conscious.

Resistance quadrants

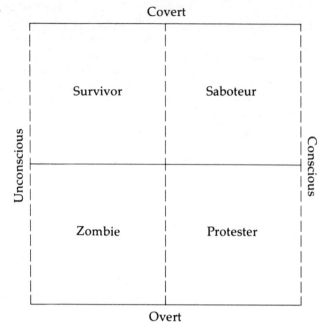

Covert

Survivor	Saboteur

Unconscious | | | Conscious

Zombie	Protester

Overt

Covert and conscious: the saboteur
These resisters undermine change while pretending to support it. Some
are motivated simply by a wish to minimize disruption and discomfort.
They believe that by verbally supporting the change and then doing
nothing, the initiative will go away. There are others who have a more
sinister motive. These individuals intend to sabotage the company or an
individual's plans for their own gain. While this is a far less frequent
occurrence than the tactic of ignoring responsibility, it is a strong
possibility within highly competitive environments.

Covert and unconscious: the survivor
These resisters don't realize that they are undermining change. They
often do not know that they are failing to meet targets or even understand the implications of their behaviour. Their activities are undetected
because higher profile projects screen or mask them. They simply soldier
on, getting the job done in the way they know how to do it. When their
lack of adaptation to change is discovered, they are as surprised and
disappointed as anyone in management. They often believe they are
doing a good job and feel discouraged by the wasted effort.

Overt and unconscious: the zombie
These resisters are an extreme case of the survivor. They are so accus-
tomed to acting in a certain way that they seem unable to change. While
they verbally agree to do whatever is asked of them, they have neither
the will nor the ability to create the change. Gradually and openly, they
revert to their former patterns of behaviour. While they realize that they
are not doing what they agreed to do, they mysteriously do not regard

this as resistance. They are simply avoiding the change until they are reminded once again that they must alter their behaviour.

Overt and conscious: the protester

These resisters believe that their refusal to change makes a positive contribution to the company. An alternative title given by some managers to this extreme group would be 'pain in the neck'. Protester resisters never seem to rest when pointing out the failings of a change. On the positive side, they serve to protect company tradition and discourage rash or sudden change. On balance, these are the easiest and certainly the most interesting kind of resisters to manage. Their resistance is not only open, but they are able to discuss their position clearly and rationally.

How to use the resistance quadrants

The four quadrants can be used to organize information about resistance. As examples of resistant behaviour emerge, these can be analysed to decide their position on the matrix. Is the behaviour covert, overt, conscious or unconscious? A tick can be placed on the appropriate area of the chart. The answers guide decisions about how to respond. Unconscious actions, either covert or overt, require managers initially to help their colleagues become aware of what they are doing and why. This can be done by asking them whether they understand the nature of the change. A series of questions could include:

- What do you believe is the goal of the change?
- What benefit does it bring the company?
- How do your actions contribute to the goal?
- If there is a gap between your actions and those which are planned for the change, how do *we* bridge that?

This approach avoids accusation. Unconscious behaviour requires education, rather than punishment. This applies to both the zombie and the survivor. After resisters become conscious of what they are doing, then it can be discovered whether they actually support the change.

Conscious behaviour which is overt should be managed by encouraging debate. The five analysis questions described in the next section guide these discussions. When resistance is conscious and covert, open debate is also recommended. In this case, though, managers should discover whether there is agreement about the end-goal for change. Ask those who *seem* to resist the change in a covert way to explain their actions in terms of their agreement to a common end-goal. It is appropriate to avoid accusation and judgement at this stage. Until it is completely clear that resistant behaviour is motivated by sabotage, moderate reactions from management are in order.

Causes of resistance: diagnosis

Five diagnostic questions

Understanding the cause of resistance allows creation of a management strategy to deal with it. There are five common causes of resistance. In the most serious cases, all five can exist together. These are:

- lack of belief that there is a serious need for change
- different descriptions of the need for change
- no agreement about goals for change
- lack of belief that the goal is attainable
- no confidence in the manager of change.

Recognizing the source of resistance guides the development of better understanding. This marks a return to the previous chapter's point about appreciating differences. Resistance results from differences: whether ideas, motives, plans, or priorities. When leaders accept the fact that members of their team all have different points of view, they work to integrate these differences and therefore minimize potential resistance. This is a vital step for the resolution of resistance: appreciate differences, understand its causes and so create resolution.

The five sources of resistance can be formulated into diagnostic questions. Managers of change can use these questions to begin the process of discovering what has specifically provoked resistance to change. If the answer to any one of the five questions is 'no', then resistance should be anticipated. Even if every circumstance associated with a change project appears to be going well, a 'no' answer means that there are potential problems.

These are the five diagnostic questions:

1 Do those people who are asked to implement the change realize that it is based on a serious need?
2 Do those involved describe or understand the need in the same way?
3 Is there a common end-goal for change to which everyone agrees?
4 Does everyone believe the goal is attainable and helps the company?
5 Is there unanimous confidence in the person selected to manage the change?

Once a potential source of resistance is identified, managers can encourage the debate of the issues surrounding that identified source. They can also consider other courses of action related to addressing this. Particularly if colleagues have unconsciously withheld their support, they need guidance to discover for themselves what is behind their resistance. The importance of identifying potential sources of resistance can be illustrated by the following example.

A team of five marketing managers meet to decide a strategy for launching their company's new product. Three of them worked closely together on a different launch the year before. The fourth team member is newly hired from a rival company and the fifth recently lost a bid for a higher level post within the company. The initial team meetings are completely dominated by the three colleagues. Although the fourth member offers ideas, these are quickly discarded by the first three. The fifth member is almost silent throughout every session.

The designated leader is one of the three well acquainted colleagues. The emphasis during the meetings is generation of ideas and discussion of feasibility. Because all of the suggestions come from just three of the members, the leader needs to be aware of potential resistance from the other two members. Although it is possible that the project will go smoothly, it is more likely that the two 'outsiders' will resist cooperating with the project decisions once they are made.

This could take the form of absenteeism from team meetings, slow completion of delegated tasks, damaging remarks outside the group about the leader's competence from the two 'outside' members, and many other resistant forms of behaviour. The two potentially resistant members can argue with good reason that they never agreed to either the project's goals or its direction. Because of this, they can question the validity of the decisions made by the other three.

An effective team leader encourages discussion so that the team develops a mutual understanding of needs, goals and direction for the project. If there is a lack of agreement about these essentials, then decisions can be undermined or seriously questioned later. Exploring the five potential sources of resistance before final decisions are made can bring to light potential misunderstandings. This process almost ensures the avoidance of unconscious resistance. The key word here is 'almost' because when dealing with people there are never any guarantees.

Each of the diagnostic questions provides a tool for managing resistance. Additional methods can support these tools. The following sections present ideas to encourage exploration of each question.

Do those people who are asked to implement the change realize that it is based on a serious need?

Discussion

Resistance results from this source often when background information about the change is limited to a few people. Those implementing the new ideas do not know the wider context for the need to change. Arguments against change that occur when there is disagreement about serious need include:

- what we have now works just fine
- this is just another 'flavour of the month'
- management never knows what they want
- this means lots of work and nothing to show for it.

Those who resist the change see the new ideas from a different perspective than those who initiate the change. Managers who wish to resolve this resistance issue should provide ample background information about the origins of the change. This is where a healthy communication system reaps rewards for company leaders. Having announced change, they can also present clearly why it is crucial to the company and therefore to its employees. The best way to manage this source of resistance is through accurate information and readiness to listen to all feedback.

Resistance benefits

A major benefit from this resistance is rediscovery of current company strengths. Colleagues who question the need for change emphasize and see benefits in what they are already doing. Their point of view should be thoroughly reviewed. There may be unnecessary features of the change or aspects which repeat current activities. All of this should be explored.

Do those involved describe or understand the need for change in the same way?

Discussion

Resistance results from this source when there is a wide range of backgrounds and experiences among the implementors of change. While they all recognize serious need, they frame the problem differently. The solutions they would each choose are based on their individual interpretation of the facts. Arguments against change that occur when those involved describe the need for change differently include:

• this solution misses the point entirely
• personal whim has no place in business
• that idea accomplishes nothing
• a serious problem needs a better solution.

Those who resist change believe that the chosen solution emphasizes the wrong features of the problem. They believe the change is shortsighted, narrow, and of limited value. This is because they bring different insights to the problem. Discussions based on this diagnostic question should solicit specific suggestions to improve the proposal for change. These would include alternatives to it as well as ideas which build on the proposal.

Resistance benefits

Exploring this source of resistance can generate a fresh approach to the chosen course of action. This can enhance a plan for change considerably. When a change team has a variety of perspectives readily available, its members can only benefit. There is a brainstorming technique which suggests that each problem-solver assumes a different identity before generating new ideas. These identities can include: a lion tamer, deep sea diver, police constable, etc. Participants seek to solve the problem through the different eyes of these various identities. It may be a good idea for leaders of change to insist that their team each take a turn describing the need for change in a new and different way.

Is there a common end-goal for change to which everyone agrees?

Discussion

Resistance results from this source when change occurs in highly competitive environments. Resisters in this case are unlikely to admit that they have different end-goals. Instead, they pursue private plans to achieve individual objectives. At times, this serves the company's end-goal, but often it does not. On those occasions when differences about goals are expressed, these usually serve special interests.

Resistance also occurs from this source when company leaders have not presented clear goals. Employees can justifiably argue that they believed they were working for company goals only to discover that they have wasted their best effort. Arguments against change that occur when end-goals differ include:

• management is weak and vacillating
• why don't they tell us what they really want?
• my private end-goal is to serve my own interests
• this new goal breaks commitments made in the past.

Resistance benefits

An indirect benefit from this cause of resistance is further clarification of the end-goal. If this has been vague or undefined, resistance can lead to a revised goal statement and renewed commitment to it.

Does everyone believe the goal is attainable and helps the company?

Discussion

Resistance results from this source when there are different beliefs about the company's available resources and the existence of threats from the environment. This leads to disagreement about the feasibility of any goal. Arguments against change that occur when there is disagreement that a goal is attainable include:

• this is another ivory tower scheme
• we don't have the resources available for this
• this change leaves us open to threats from outside
• this change does us more harm than good.

Initiators of change find this kind of resistance very difficult to manage because withheld support seems to be a way of questioning their competence as agents of change. In fact, particularly in this case, those who resist change have the good of the company at heart. Their cautious stance is based on a wish to conserve present levels of success. If the leaders of change can keep their sense of humour, discussions about the cause of resistance can directly strengthen innovation. This kind of resistor is frequently an expert with a different point of view to offer.

Resistance benefits

Discussion of this resistance issue leads to analysis of company strengths, weaknesses, opportunities and threats. All of this information, drawn from resisters' different perspectives, is very valuable for planners of change. A cautious review of plans for change should address feedback from these sources.

Is there unanimous confidence in the person selected to manage the change?

Discussion

Resistance results from this source for several different reasons. First, resisters may believe that the project is too large in scope for one person to manage. Second, the person chosen may be inexperienced or have a poor management record. Third, those with a special interest in the change may believe the manager should be drawn from their own area of expertise. Arguments against change that occur when there is a lack of confidence in its manager include:

- who is this person anyway?
- failure follows this person like a shadow
- this change needs specialist leadership
- there is no way that I am following this lead.

Poor management is the major cause of business failure. When there is a serious lack of confidence in leaders of change, people have a difficult time agreeing with their ideas. Those who resist change need to be encouraged to see the selected manager in a positive light. Adequate information should be published to explain the choice. If serious doubts remain, then a schedule of report dates should be set, with agreed performance standards.

Resistance benefits

When there is a lack of confidence in the person chosen to manage change, this can be turned to advantage. Interim goals for achievement are likely to be willingly accepted and greater interest shown in monitoring the progress of the change. All of this adds up to a greater sense of shared responsibility for making change happen.

Problem—
analysis—
discussion

Problem   The original partners of a well-known legal firm created a legacy of conservative image, strong client base and fairly rigid management procedures. Their founding principles strongly influenced succeeding generations of partners to maintain stability and avoid change. The superior quality of the firm's work was its means of promoting the practice. This approach served the firm well until the late 'seventies, when competition for clients in their firm's area of specialism increased dramatically.

Newly forming firms were actively seeking business through subtle forms of promotion. As a result, they gained clients and prestige within the community. Although the firm described in this problem maintained their currently engaged clients, they gained little new business. During the boom years of the 'eighties, the firm continued to hold steady, but did not grow to the extent of their rivals.

For several years, the grandson of one of the founding members and its youngest partner, pressed his two equity partners to expand the firm's services. His partners resisted his suggestions as unwise and out of keeping with the firm's image. They even accused him of following personal taste rather than professional interest.

In the early 'nineties, the recession's effect on its clients' businesses began to have an indirect impact on the firm's income. The youngest partner once again stressed the need to increase the firm's revenue by offering a wider range of services. Even as he offered these arguments, the firm's major client, a construction company, went into receivership, owing the firm more than £300 000 in accumulated fees.

None of the partners were aware of the extensive, uncollected billings or of the increasing financial distress of their client. The senior partner, now in his seventies, had been responsible for the firm's administration and financial control. When the three partners met to discuss their present situation, he proposed that they modernize their billing and collection systems. He offered to reorganize the firm as a means of minimizing the effects of the recession.

The third partner suggested, instead, that they hire an outside consultant to advise them on a subtle marketing strategy. He stressed that they could increase their client list by emphasizing high quality service and their number of satisfied clients. Feeling very impatient with his colleagues, he said that developing new services or conducting a management audit would be an indulgence of personal whim in a time of crisis.

Analysis   *Imagine that you are a neutral observer to this group of three partners. Please respond to the following questions from that point of view.*

1 What do you believe is the source of resistance?
2 Referring to the resistance quadrants (page 118), where should each of these partners be placed?
3 Can you propose a goal for change for this group?
4 Recognizing that there is a four-stage method for change available to you, how would you proceed?
5 How would you seek to gain agreement among the partners for a plan for change?

Discussion   Each of the three partners has different definitions of what needs to change within their firm. All three are correct. Their task is to listen carefully to each other toward integrating their partners' ideas with their own. From this, a stronger, better solution emerges, based on three different perspectives.

The main source of resistance is the different priorities each partner brings to the practice. The youngest member gains the most from ensuring that the practice has long-term success. The eldest is near retirement and gains least from change. The third partner shares the priorities of the eldest partner, seeing advantage in tradition and disadvantage in change. Their collective challenge is recognizing that the interests of all three partners are equally valid.

On the resistance matrix, the eldest would be placed in the covert/ unconscious sector, the 'survivor'. He is unlikely to describe his own behaviour as resistance; rather, he sees no need to change. The middle-aged partner could be placed in the overt/conscious sector, the 'protester'. He makes a virtue of resisting the ideas of his two partners. His own proposal is to promote what the firm already does. Traditionalists often find themselves in this camp. They believe that by upholding tradition, they endorse a valuable part of company identity.

The youngest partner in this example is the agent of change. Therefore it is difficult to place him on the matrix. When he is resisting change himself, he would be likely to express covert/unconscious behaviour, like the eldest partner. This is indicated by his acceptance of his partners' resistance over a period of years. It is the cash crisis which leads to their discussion of change, not this partner's ideas about expanding the firm's services.

Before making any plans, they should explore all three of their suggestions. First, they should compare their range of services with those of competing firms and ask themselves how they can improve what they do. This evaluation and their subsequent decisions would influence their choices about marketing. Finally, the firm's reorganization would directly contribute to the effectiveness of the other two initiatives.

It is essential for them to take time to reach agreement on the desired end-result. They should not assume that their colleagues envision the future as they do themselves. This is rarely the case. Disagreements and resistance often result from lack of communication or an inability to believe that a colleague's goal can be achieved.

Finally, one of the partners should take responsibility for creating change. He must have the full confidence and endorsement of the other two partners. If there are doubts, these must be expressed and taken seriously. To minimize further resistance, evaluation stages should be established in advance. The partner in charge would then report fully to the other partners on a scheduled basis. This allows debate and continued contributions from all three.

Summary

This chapter explores the nature of resistance to change and recommends strategies to resolve it. First, managers need to recognize resistance, distinguishing minor disagreements from potential conflicts. Two complementary approaches are suggested for an analysis of resistance: to examine categories of resistant behaviour and to explore possible causes of resistance.

A double matrix of unconscious to conscious motivation and covert to overt behaviour provides the means to categorize resistance. This matrix produces four quadrants with four resistant types of behaviour: the saboteur, the protester, the zombie, and the survivor. Causes of resistance are explored using five diagnostic questions. Recommendations are made to managers for resolving resistance, once its cause is discovered.

Selected reading

Argyris, Chris, *Strategy, Change and Defensive Routines*. Boston: Putnam, 1985.
Block, Peter, *The Empowered Manager*. San Francisco: Jossey-Bass, 1987.
Eisenberg, Eric M. and Witten, Marsha G., 'Reconsidering Openness in Organizational Communication', *Academy of Management Review*, **12**, 3, 1987, pp 418–26.
Kanter, Rosebeth M., *A Tale of 'O': On Being Different in an Organization*. New York: Harper & Row, 1980.
O'Connor, Carol A., 'Organizational Impasse: Diagnosis and Intervention', *Management Decisions*, **30**, 3, 1992, pp 32–9.

Conclusion

Change is an ongoing part of life. It occurs regardless of its participants' wishes. Fighting the inevitable or pretending that change can be avoided is not only an impossible task but also inhibits the opportunity of influencing its outcome. Wisdom suggests, instead, accepting change as the catalyst for producing new things from old.

This book recommends *working with* change in this way. It promotes skills, attitudes and a method which allow a pro-active approach for managing change. It also suggests that qualities of courage, humour, respect and attentive listening go a long way toward creating a climate for successful change, in business and in life.

Appendix: addresses

These are the company addresses of those managers who are interviewed in this book's case studies.

Cathy Carter Duncan
Seymour Duncan Research
601 Pine Avenue
Santa Barbara, CA 93117
USA

Ian Halliday
The Prudential Assurance Company Limited
Forbury House
18–20 The Forbury
Reading Berks RG1 3ES
UK

Tina Kaplan
Human Resources
Scandinavian Airlines
STODH
Frösundaviks Alle
S16187 Stockholm
Sweden

Anthony Lewis
Ford Motor Company
Warley Central Office
Eagle Way
Brentwood Essex CM13 3BW
UK

Daniel Ofman
Kern Konsult
Beerensteinerlaan 24
1406 NS Bussum
Netherlands

Paull Robathan
Infact Limited
46 Clerkenwell Close
London EC1R 0AT
UK

Dr Stephen Tanner
Life Administration Home Service Division
The Prudential Assurance Company Limited
Forbury House
18–20 The Forbury
Reading Berks RG1 3ES
UK

This is the address of the developer of the
team building model presented on page 104.

George and Judith Brown and Associates
2141 Ridge Lane
Santa Barbara, CA 93103
USA

Carol A. O'Connor
Vision in Practice, Management Consultants
23D Belsize Park Gardens
London NW3 4JH
UK

Bibliography

Argenti, John, *Predicting Corporate Failure*. London: Institute of Chartered Accountants in England and Wales, 1984.

Argenti, John, *Practical Corporate Planning* (rev. ed). London: Unwin Hyman, 1989.

Argyle, M. (ed.), *Social Skills and Work*. London: Methuen, 1981.

Argyris, Chris, *Strategy, Change and Defensive Routines*. Boston: Putnam, 1985.

Barnett, John H. and Wilsted, William D., *Strategic Management: Text and Concepts*. Boston: PWS-Kent Publishing, 1989.

Bennis, Warren and Nanus, Burt, *Leaders: The Strategies for Taking Charge*. New York: Harper & Row, 1985.

Block, Peter, *The Empowered Manager*. San Francisco: Jossey-Bass, 1987.

Burn, James M., *Leadership*. New York: Harper & Row, 1978.

Croon, Peter, *Strategy and Strategy Creation*. Rotterdam: Rotterdam University Press, 1974.

de Bono, Edward, *Lateral Thinking for Management*. New York: Penguin, 1982.

de Bono, Edward, *The Mechanism of Mind*. London: Penguin, 1990.

Edelman, Murray, *The Symbolic Uses of Politics*. Chicago: University of Illinois Press, 1967.

Eisenberg, Eric M. and Witten, Marsha G., 'Reconsidering Openness in Organizational Communication', *Academy of Management Review*, **12**, 3, 1987, 418–26.

Gainer, Leila J., 'Making the Competitive Connection', *Training and Development Journal*. September 1989, S1–30.

Galbraith, John K., *The New Industrial State*. London: Hamilton, 1967.

Guba, Egon G. and Lincoln, Yvonna S., *Effective Evaluation*. San Francisco: Jossey-Bass, 1981.

Halperin, Samuel, *A Guide for the Powerless and Those Who Do Not Know Their Own Power*. Washington DC: Institute for Educational Leadership, 1981.

Hamilton, David, *Beyond the Numbers Game*. Basingstoke: Macmillan, 1977.

Handy, Charles, *Understanding Organizations*. London: Penguin, 1985.

Handy, Charles, *Waiting for the Mountain to Move*. London: Hutchinson, 1990.

Kanter, Rosebeth Moss, *A Tale of 'O': On Being Different in an Organization*. New York: Harper & Row, 1980.

Kanter, Rosebeth Moss, *The Change Masters: Corporate Entrepreneurs at Work*. London: Allen & Unwin, 1985.

Kanter, Rosebeth Moss, *When Giants Learn To Dance*. London: Unwin Hyman, 1990.

London, Manuel, *Change Agents: New Roles and Innovation Strategies for Human Resource Professionals*. San Francisco: Jossey-Bass, 1988.

March, J. and Olsen, J., *Ambiguity and Choice in Organizations*. Bergen, Norway: Universitetsforlaget, 1979.

Merry, Uri and Brown, George I., *Neurotic Behavior of Organizations*. Cleveland, OH: Gardner, 1986.

Miles, R.E. and Snow, C.C., *Organizational Strategy, Structure, and Process*. New York: McGraw-Hill, 1978.

Mintzberg, Henry and Quinn, James B., *The Strategy Process* (2nd ed.). Englewood Cliffs, NJ: Prentice-Hall, 1991.

Naisbitt, John, *Megatrends: Ten New Directions Transforming Our Lives*. London: MacDonald, 1984.

O'Connor, Carol A., 'Organizational Impasse: Diagnosis and Intervention'. *Management Decisions*, **30**, 3, 1992, 32–9.

Pearce, John A. II and Robinson, Richard B. Jr, *Strategic Management: Strategic Formulation and Implementation* (2nd ed.). Homewood, IL: Irwin, 1985.

Pearce, John A. II and Robinson, Richard B. Jr, *Corporate Stategies: A Selection of Readings from Business Week*. New York: McGraw-Hill, 1986.

Perloff, Robert (ed.), *Evaluator Interventions: Pros and Cons*. London: Sage, 1979.

Porter, Michael, *Competitive Advantage: Creating and Sustaining Superior Performance*. New York: The Free Press, 1985.

Reich, R.B., 'The Real Economy', *The Atlantic Monthly*. February 1991, 35–52.

Sloan Management Review, *Planning Strategies that Work*. Oxford: Oxford University Press, 1987.

Smith, Kenneth and Berg, David, *Paradoxes in Group Life*. San Francisco: Jossey-Bass, 1987.

Smith, Nick L. (ed.), *New Techniques for Evaluation*. London: Sage, 1981.

Stevenson, Howard H., 'Defining Corporate Strengths and Weaknesses', *Sloan Management Review*. Spring 1976, 51–68.

White, Ralph K. and Lippitt, Ronald, *Autocracy and Democracy: an Experimental Inquiry*. New York: Harper & Brothers, 1960.

Index

Further titles in the McGraw-Hill Training Series

THE BUSINESS OF TRAINING
Achieving Success in Changing World Markets
Trevor Bentley   ISBN 0-07-707328-2

EVALUATING TRAINING EFFECTIVENESS
Translating Theory into Practice
Peter Bramley   ISBN 0-07-707331-2

DEVELOPING EFFECTIVE TRAINING SKILLS
Tony Pont   ISBN 0-07-707383-5

MAKING MANAGEMENT DEVELOPMENT WORK
Achieving Success in the Nineties
Charles Margerison   ISBN 0-07-707382-7

MANAGING PERSONAL LEARNING AND CHANGE
A Trainer's Guide
Neil Clark   ISBN 0-07-707344-4

HOW TO DESIGN EFFECTIVE TEXT-BASED OPEN
LEARNING:
A Modular Course
Nigel Harrison   ISBN 0-07-707355-X

HOW TO DESIGN EFFECTIVE COMPUTER-BASED
TRAINING:
A Modular Course
Nigel Harrison   ISBN 0-07-707354-1

HOW TO SUCCEED IN EMPLOYEE DEVELOPMENT
Moving from Vision to Results
Ed Moorby   ISBN 0-07-707459-9

USING VIDEO IN TRAINING AND EDUCATION
Ashly Pinnington   ISBN 0-07-707384-3

TRANSACTIONAL ANALYSIS FOR TRAINERS
Julie Hay   ISBN 0-07-707470-X

SELF-DEVELOPMENT
A Facilitator's Guide
Mike Pedler and
David Megginson   ISBN 0-07-707460-2

DEVELOPING WOMEN THROUGH TRAINING
A Practical Handbook
Liz Willis,
Jenny Daisley   ISBN 0-707-707566-8